7000 00

Dealing
with

DIFFICULT SPOUSES & CHILDREN

ROBERTA CAVA

How to handle difficult family problems

 CAVA MANAGEMENT CONSULTING SERVICES

_____

Canadian Cataloguing in Publication Data

Cava, Roberta
    Dealing with Difficult Spouses & Children

ISBN 01895632-16-1

Printed and bound in Canada.

Cava Management Consulting Services,
#1201 - 12319 Jasper Avenue,
Edmonton, Alberta Canada, T5N 4A7

Phone: (403) 482-7014
FAX: (403) 488-2747

DEDICATION

Dedicated to the participants of my seminar
DEALING WITH DIFFICULT PEOPLE who have
kindly passed on their ideas, so others might
benefit from their knowledge.

Contents

* courtesy to others
* too much to do!
* finding the right child care
* negative tapes
* disciplining when angry
* to spank or not to spank?
* touching children
* why won't she listen to me?

Chapter Nine: **PROBLEMS WITH CHILDREN**   129

* nervous habits
* late pregnancy
* terrible twos
* hyperactive child
* decisions, decisions
* tantrums
* missing child
* favouritism
* dealing with bullies
* shy child
* rejected child
* change in behaviour
* manipulative child
* tattling
* lying
* phoney illnesses
* sex stereotyping
* food hassles
* daydreaming
* sleep-overs
* twins
* summer vacation
* separation
* death of a sibling

ACKNOWLEDGEMENTS

My gratitude is extended to the thousands of participants of my seminars who contributed ideas on how THEY handled their difficult spouses and children.

The Canadian Mental Health Association, who allowed me to quote directly from their information, are sincerely thanked for their valuable contribution.

Special thanks goes to my friend Phil Sutton, who kept my computer running by always being available at a moment's notice, and to my male friends who gave their valuable input to the section on male/female communication.

INTRODUCTION

This publication is a sequel to my book DIFFICULT PEOPLE - **How to Deal With Impossible Clients, Bosses and Employees,** 1990 (Key Porter Books). Rather than gearing it towards those in the work-force, I've slanted this one towards spouses and children who may be, upset, irate, rude, impatient, emotional, persistent or just plain aggressive.

These difficult people may try to manipulate you into doing things you don't want to do, keep you from doing the things you want to do, try to give you negative feelings about yourself, or make you lose your cool.

This book is not a cure, and I'm not presumptuous enough to think I have all the answers. What you will gain however, are alternatives to the way you're presently dealing with problems, to give you the option of trying plan "B" and "C," when your plan "A" doesn't work.

The main focus of this book is to help you realize that, though you can try to change someone else's behaviour, in reality, you have little control over the actions of others. What you DO have control of, is YOUR reaction to other people's negative behaviour.

Unfortunately most of us are on automatic pilot and react the same negative way, to the same kind of negative situations, whether that way worked in the past or not. This leads to feelings of frustration, helplessness and the belief that our life is out-of-control. Then, because we don't feel we're in control of situations, our self-confidence deteriorates.

Many serious problems surface when men and women try to communicate with each other. Their different communication styles are not readily understood by the opposite gender, so misunderstandings and misinterpretation of both verbal and non-verbal messages can be the norm. I've devoted a complete chapter to this perplexing communication problem.

How do I know my techniques really work? More than 25,000 participants (internationally) who have attended my DEALING WITH DIFFICULT PEOPLE seminars endorse the techniques described in this book and use them often. Many have taken time to write to me after their seminars to offer their wisdom and have given me additional tips on how they handled their difficult spouses and children.

What will you gain? You'll learn techniques that will enable you to remain calm, gain a more positive attitude, and maintain your emotional well-being when faced with life's negative situations. Your self-confidence level will rise, and you'll be in control when dealing with difficult spouses, and children.

Watch for future sequels entitled:

* DEALING WITH DIFFICULT RELATIVES AND IN-LAWS,

* DEALING WITH DIFFICULT FRIENDS AND NEIGHBOURS, and

* DEALING WITH DIFFICULT PROFESSIONAL AND TRADESPEOPLE.

CHAPTER 1
EVALUATE YOUR ACTIONS

Controlling your moods

Before you can tackle difficult family members, it's essential that you have *your* act together. Could your actions or behaviour be a trigger for the other person's difficult behaviour? Could you have done or said something that started the difficult encounter?

Are you a moody person yourself? Do you have mood swings that affect what kind of day you have? Are you up one hour, down the next - up one day, down the next? If you're normally a moody person, you've probably allowed others' behaviour and actions to affect your day.

Every day we're faced with negative situations that cause negative emotions. Some emotions they initiate make us feel:

- angry	- anxious	- ashamed
- depressed	- disappointed	- embarrassed
- hopeless	- helpless	- manipulated
- frustrated	- guilty	- hurt
- victimized	- humiliated	- foolish
- ignored	- inferior	- insecure
- intimidated	- jealous	- nervous
- silly	- confused	- uncomfortable
- rejected	- resentful	- restricted
- sad	- stupid	- suspicious
- tense	- troubled	- uneasy
- upset or	- worried	- hesitant

Most of us react to situations that happen around us - whether they're good or bad. For instance, someone throws an angry remark at you, a friend makes a hurting comment or someone tries to make you feel guilty. Can you maintain control over your emotions and your reactions under those circumstances? Or do you react almost automatically to the negative stimulus from others and retaliate, feel hurt, or feel guilty?

I'm sure you'll agree, it's the little annoyances that end up ruining your day. So if you can learn how to handle the little annoyances, you'll have more energy and stamina to handle the really big ones.

If you believe that outside circumstances cause unhappiness, and that you have no control over this unhappiness - you're wrong. Actually, outside forces and events cannot be harmful unless *you allow them to affect you*. Happiness comes largely from within a person. While external events may irritate or annoy you, you still have control over how you respond.

You relinquish an important part of your self-esteem, if you find that others dominate whether you have a good or bad day. How do you feel when you face a negative situation? What happens to your self-esteem level when you're not in control of situations? Does it stay intact, or is it bruised by the other person's negative actions? This is what keeps us off-balance. When we feel in control of situations, we feel as if both our feet stay firmly planted. But, if we react badly to someone's negative behaviour, we may find ourselves losing that control.

If you can't maintain control of how you react when others behave badly, you owe it to yourself to learn how to change your reactions. Remember, *you* decide whether someone's angry remark should upset you or not. *You* allow yourself to feel hurt when someone is unkind to you. And *you* choose to feel guilty whether it's warranted or not.

Do you blame others for how you feel? When you make comments such as, *"He always makes me feel so inferior."* Or, *"She makes me so mad when she . . . "* Or, our own self-talk says, *"You goofed again. How dumb can you be? Won't you ever learn?"* You're allowing others (and yourself) to ruin your day. By allowing yourself to feel badly about situations, or take on guilt you don't deserve, you're giving **yourself** a bad day. Face it - you're going to gain nothing by blaming others for the way you feel.

I'm sure you've faced a day where everything seems to go wrong! In fact, you wish you could go back to bed (and it's only 10:00 a.m.)! How you react to this kind of day, often determines the outcome of it. Most people respond by saying, *"Oh boy. It's going to be one of those days!"* They expect the rest of the day to be terrible - and of course it is! They set themselves up for a bad day, and are rewarded accordingly.

If you find yourself facing the kind of day where three or four negative situations occur, have a talk with yourself. Instead of saying *"It's going to be one of those days!"* say, *"Thank goodness I got that out of the way!"* What you're doing is telling yourself that the rest of the day is going to be better (because all the bad stuff has already happened). Try changing your attitude from negative to positive when you're having a bad day, and see if your day doesn't turn around.

Handling your emotions

When others become irate, rude, impatient or angry, you probably become upset yourself. The first step towards keeping your cool is to change your responses to negative occurrences. My life changed when I realized that I could choose how I reacted when faced with difficult situations. I could either *take* the bad feelings thrust upon me by others, or simply *not take* them. I accomplished this by stopping my defense mechanism from kicking in. This is the same defensive reaction that cavemen and cavewomen had. They prepared themselves mentally and physically to either stand and fight the dinosaur, or run like crazy in the opposite direction.

Today, the same reaction occurs when we're faced with dangerous or negative situations. Stop for a moment and ask yourself what mental and physical reactions happen to you when someone is angry with you, is hurting you with their comments or is trying to make you feel guilty about something.

More often than not, your defense mechanism kicks in and you have some of the following symptoms:

* rapid pulse
* pounding heart

* increased perspiration
* tightened stomach muscles

3

* shortness of breath	* tensing of leg & arm muscles
* gritting of teeth	* clenching of the jaw
* inability to sit still	* raging thoughts
* blood pressure rises	* excessive gripping emotions
* digestion slows down	* faster breathing
* loss of patience	* person becomes jumpy
* clammy feeling	* extremities cold
* body trembles	* head and stomach aches
* more emotional	* nervous stomach
* rashes and hives	* hyper-ventilates
* insomnia	* loss of or increased appetite

The first step I took towards becoming more immune to others' barbs and difficult behaviour was to identify when my defense mechanism was triggered. I recognized that I was mentally and physically preparing to defend myself. My reactions were - my heart pounded, my thoughts raced, I'd feel the blood rushing to my face, and my muscles would stiffen (mostly my stomach muscles). Do you have similar reactions? If not, what happens to you when you feel that *your* defense mechanism has been triggered?

As soon as I identify this reaction in myself, I stop (this takes only a split second) and question whether I'm reacting correctly to the negative situation. Nine times out of ten, I recognize that I'm over-reacting or am allowing *myself* to feel badly.

I also recognize that my self-esteem was lower when I faced situations where I didn't feel "in control." I'd feel incompetent when I was in the throes of difficult situations. When I learned how to control my reactions, I could maintain a high self-esteem level. This allowed me to direct my energy towards positive, rather than negative use. Instead of running away, feeling hurt or defending myself, I dealt with the situation.

When I learned this simple technique, I found I had far more control over my everyday moods. Gone were the roller coaster mood swings of the past. Other people didn't decide what kind of day I'd have - I did! You too can have this control.

The ability to master this skill is easier than you might believe. All it takes is practice - but you *can* do it if you set your mind to it! As soon as you feel yourself showing signs of stress and feel the need to defend yourself - stop and practice my technique.

If you don't turn off your defense mechanism, you'll allow others to give you their negative feelings. If you allow negative feelings to go in, they rumble around, but have to be released somehow. And how do these negative feelings get out - you give them to someone or something else. You yell back at or are nasty to the next person you see, you kick the dog or even throw something.

Sound familiar? Why are you allowing someone else to trigger these responses? Remember, you can't control other people's behaviour, but you CAN control how you respond to their negative behaviour. By accepting their anger, you've given them control over the next few minutes, hours, or even days of your life.

Is this person worthy of having that much control over your emotions? In most instances, I think you'll decide a definite, NO.

Of course, there will be exceptions where this technique won't work because the situations are so serious such as:

* Having an accident or being seriously ill
* Getting fired from your job unjustly, or
* Someone you know is seriously ill or dying.

But these are exceptions. Most everyday moods and reactions you *can* control.

How to "keep your cool"

Think of a situation where someone you knew was in a bad mood. Instead of taking the time to analyze their behaviour and realize that they're not going to be easy to talk to, you forge ahead with conversation. You respond negatively because of their actions, allow their comments to effect you, and end up with hurt feelings.

Why did you allow this to happen? Later they'll likely apologize to you about their behaviour. Watch your timing;

5

anticipate others' responses, and don't push them when the timing is wrong. Don't allow the person's angry comments to affect you, and let them change your relationship with them.

However, if this person is in a bad mood most of the time, you shouldn't have to "walk on eggs" and watch every word you say when communicating with them. If this is the case, confront the person and explain your aversion to his or her behaviour. Try using the feedback technique (see Chapter 3).

Keeping your cool under fire takes concentrated effort. If you're quick to become angry, focus your energies on stopping your automatic defense mechanism. Instead, try the following tactics:

* Tune into your feelings. I feel sad . . . unhappy . . .
* Narrow down or find the cause of your feelings. Did they go back on their word? Did they let you down or break a trust?
* Try to understand why you felt angry, sad, unhappy, fearful etc. Were they accusing you unfairly? Or did you deserve their behaviour because of something you did or did not do?
* Deal with your feelings realistically, share feelings with the person that upset you - communicate, don't shut them out.
     "When you yell at me, I freeze up and can't respond the way I want to."
* Take a walk. Use your adrenalin effectively by aiming your energy towards constructive activities. Determine why they did or said what they did. How should you deal with their actions? What could you say or do that would resolve the problem? Then do it.

Using logic and emotion

These two forces - logic and emotion, are at work throughout our lives. They're often pushing and pulling in opposite directions. The prevailing one may determine how we get along with others and effect our level of achievement.

As children, we remember feeling pleasure, happiness, excitement, fun, and love (positive emotions). Or we remember feeling insecure and inferior if we were compared to others. Our school grades, our prowess at sports, and our physical appearance were all carefully evaluated. This often resulted in negative behaviours such as pouting, tantrums, shouting, arguing, cursing, blaming others, spreading gossip, giving the silent treatment, showing jealousy or resentment. These negative responses seldom received favourable reactions.

Sample Situations:

Here are examples of how you could be going on "automatic pilot" when facing negative situations:

1. You allow yourself to accept others' anger

a) For example: Since your brother Lorne came home, he's been ranting and raving about the problems he's had with the car all day. He's picked you to take the blame for his problems. *"It's all your fault! You don't properly maintain the car."*
        Although you share the use of the car, you know this isn't true, and he's blaming you for something that isn't your fault. What's your natural, instinctive, reaction in this kind of situation? Is it to yell back at him? Is it to put your defenses up and prepare to retaliate with explanations about why this is *not* your fault?
        You remember my instructions to stop for a split second to determine whether you're reacting reasonably. You ask yourself why your defense mechanism kicked in? Was Lorne really mad at you - or was he mad at the situation, and you happened to be there to enable him to vent his frustrations? I think you'll agree that the latter is likely the case.
        Because he's mad at the situation (not you) why have you let your defense mechanism kick in? Is this warranted under the circumstances? He probably just needs to vent his anger and you happened to be available as a receptacle. Concentrate your efforts on seeing what's behind his blowup.
    Use empathy, put yourself in his place. Diffuse his anger at the situation, by helping him find solutions to his problem.
        Start with, *"What happened today that has you so steamed up."* Listen carefully to what he says. If he continues to try to blame you, *"You never maintain the car properly."* Tell him what you *have* done to maintain the car and ask what else you should have done. Get the dialogue going. Reply, *"What do*

*you think I should have done that would have kept the problem
from happening?"*

b) Example #2: You're driving home from work, feeling pretty
tired from a stressful day at work, and find yourself fuming
because the traffic is backed up *again.* It feels as if you spend
half your life waiting in traffic to get home. You finally get
home, stride through the living room past your children and slam
your bedroom door. You've allowed the traffic jam to get you
upset. And it doesn't stop there.

What happened to your two children who were sitting in
the living room watching TV when you strode by? They're likely
to wonder what *they* did to make you so mad. This puts them
on edge so they snap at each other during dinner. You can see
how your bad mood has a domino effect on others.

You know you're likely to face traffic jams on the way
home - it happens three out of five times - so why have you
allowed yourself to get so upset? When you were driving home,
you had a choice about how you reacted. Instead:

  (i) Try leaving work half an hour later. This may get you
     home just ten minutes later than now, but with far less
     harassment.
 (ii) Vary your work hours to stop the negatives you receive
     now.
(iii) Buy some audio cassettes that have calming music, and
     listen to them while you drive home.
(iv) Allow yourself more time to drive home.

Or, possibly your wife's hours differ from yours and
you're responsible for getting dinner started. Think of alternate
solutions. For instance, get your two teen-aged children involved
in starting or preparing dinner. This alleviates your need to rush
home from work and the hassles it causes.

If you can't arrange this, tell yourself that you won't get
distressed driving home.

2. YOU respond negatively to guilt

We live in a guilt-ridden society. We allow others to make us
feel guilty and we're very efficient at giving ourselves guilt
feelings as well. We feel guilty if we can't understand what

someone's saying on the phone or we feel guilty because we make mistakes. Identify things you've done in the past that you're not proud of. Then, instead of wallowing in guilt, learn from the experience. If an apology is needed to remove the guilt - then apologize.

a) They throw guilt at you so You allow yourself to feel guilty:

Our parents are often the ones who can give us the most effective and guilt-laden feelings. They give comments such as, *"If you loved me more, you'd come over to see me more often. "*

When others try to make you feel guilty, stop and identify what their comments really mean. Analyze whether there is truth to their comments, then act accordingly. For the parent who complained that they didn't see you often enough reply, *"Mom, why are you trying to make me feel guilty? You know I have too busy a schedule to see you more than once a week. "*

Recognize when others are manipulating you by trying to make you feel guilty. You can't change the past despite how you or they feel about it. Some parents have long memories and bring up events that happened years ago. Accept that you have the right to choose to do or be something other than what others may expect or want you to be.

For instance, insisting that there's no other profession worthwhile other than nursing (when you want to be a social worker). It's nice to have your parent's approval, but not at the risk of your feeling of self-worth. You have the right to choose how you live (providing you're not breaking the laws of the land). You also must be ready to take the consequences of your behaviour and choices. Recognize that others (your children perhaps?) have this right as well. It's unfair to force your ideas on others by trying to make the person feel guilty.

Others may try to transfer their responsibility to you or try to obtain pity from you by attempting to make you feel guilty. They make comments such as:

"I work night and day to bring home my paycheque and you reward me by . . . "

"I spent all day cooking this meal and it takes you fifteen minutes to eat it. The least you could do, is help clear the table. "

"You never call me any more. "

9

"It's 3:00 a.m. How come you're so late? Do you want me to have a heart attack?"

"If you loved me, you'd . . . "

"What will the neighbours think?"

"Do you want Grandma and Grandpa to think you're bad mannered? Get busy and write those thank-you cards."

"How can I believe you now, when you lied to me the last time you did this?"

"How can you just sit there watching your stupid football game when there's so much to do around here?"

"I stayed with your mother because of you kids."

How do you handle a person who's trying to make you feel guilty? First, identify whether their comments or statements are true. If so, deal with the issue. If the guilt is not warranted, try to establish why they're trying to manipulate you, and what they expect to gain by doing so.

In the last example, the father was trying to lay guilt on his children because he stayed in an unhappy marriage. He said, *"I stayed with your mother because of you kids."*

One son handled his father's attempt to make him feel guilty by replying, *"You're trying to make us feel responsible for your staying with Mom. Why do you feel we were responsible for that decision?"*

The father retaliated with explanations about why he stayed.

The son repeated his comment, *"Why do you feel WE were responsible for YOUR decision?"* The father finally had to admit that he had to take full responsibility for his actions, not his children.

Another example is: A stay-at-home neighbour asked Audra, a single mother, *"Why aren't you staying at home with your children?"*

Audra, *"Do you think I'd be a better mother if I stayed at home with my children and went on welfare rather than go to work to support my family?"*

"Not really, but I still think your children need you to be there for them."

"That wouldn't be practical in my case. I can't help but wonder why you're trying to make me feel guilty about my decision to return to work."

Another example: You've worked very hard painting the bathroom, and are very proud of your accomplishment. You wait patiently for recognition from members of your family. Is recognition likely to come? Typically - it isn't. What you're more likely to hear about, is a small portion of the task you did wrong (*"You missed this spot,"* or *"The paint ran here."*)

Unfortunately, if someone criticizes you, you may automatically accept their comments without question. This allows the one giving criticism to you, to control how you feel about yourself. This obviously can seriously affect your self-confidence level.

Then you may get the feeling that you *did* do a poor job, and accept the guilt feelings that accompany the criticism. Learn to evaluate the relevancy of other people's comments. Are your guilt feelings warranted? Could you be responding negatively because that's the way you've always responded in the past? Re-evaluate the situation. What type of job do you feel you did? Were you originally pleased? Why aren't you pleased now?

Don't count on others to give recognition. If they do give recognition - think of their praise as "gravy." But you don't need gravy on the potatoes every night do you? Like too much gravy (which can make you swell up), you could become swell-headed if you received praise for everything you did.

Never compete against the record of someone else. Just work to improve your record of accomplishments. The person you should be trying to please, is YOU. Most of us set high standards for ourselves. When you feel you're being shoved around psychologically, state how you feel (no apologies). The fact that others disapprove of what you do, has nothing to do with what or who you are. You're not responsible for the happiness of others - they must make themselves happy. You're responsible only for your own emotions.

b) You make yourself feel guilty:

As if others' criticism isn't bad enough, we all seem to have a little twerp inside us who loves to criticize. This voice makes

11

such comments as, *"Well, you goofed again! Can't you do anything right?"*

Since you have given a situation your best effort - that's all you can expect of yourself. For some reason society has taught us to feel guilty because we make mistakes. If you made a mistake - recognize that it's just that - a mistake and simply don't do it again. Mistakes are to learn from, and should not make us feel as if we're a failure. Stop being hypercritical and start giving yourself positive reinforcement.

If you've done a good job, mentally pat yourself on the back with such thoughts as, *"I'm really proud of how well I painted that room."*

3. <u>You</u> allow yourself to have revengeful feelings

Think of a time when someone's "done you wrong." Did you fuss and fume - vowing to make them pay for their actions? How long did it take you to plan your revenge and follow it through to completion? Did you spend years planning revenge for a perceived wrongdoing and did that hate overshadow just about everything else in your life?

A prime example is a divorced spouse who is *"going to pay him or her back for what s/he's done to me!"* These individuals have difficulty getting on with their lives, because they're so caught up in their revengeful thoughts. Some waste precious years and personal future relationships instead of getting on with their lives.

Stand back from the situation for a moment, and analyze what actually happened. Who had control over the person's time, emotions and energy while they were planning their revenge? In reality, *concentrating on getting revenge, ties the person to the wrongdoer, instead of allowing them to get on with their life!*

If you find yourself having revengeful feelings and can deal with the issue right away - do so. But if you can't deal with the wrongdoer right away, drop the issue and don't allow thoughts of "getting revenge" to enter your mind. Remind yourself, that as long as you're dwelling on the other person's negative acts, you're still giving him or her control of your life. Is that person worthy of having this kind of impact on your life? I doubt it!

4. You allow yourself to feel stressed

We may find ourselves feeling stressed when we face an over-load of work. If we can't handle our time properly, it makes us more stressed. The more stressed we become, the more trouble we have dealing with our difficult people and situations.

If this is your problem, eliminate some of your stress. Take a time management course or read time management books to help you choose priorities. Spend time on *your* priorities. Make *To Do* lists, so you'll know exactly how many tasks you can handle in a day.

5. You allow yourself to feel depressed

Normally, some important loss triggers depression. You may feel despondent when you lose items of value, friends, health, promotions, income and value as a human being. As you mature, you'll lose many items of value - jobs, income, prestige, friends and health. You may be in a home situation that's not suitable. Your depression can actually be anger you turn against yourself because you may feel helpless to do anything to change your situation.

Or, you may allow yourself to feel depressed for no other reason except that it's Monday morning. You find yourself energized Friday afternoon, but feel down or depressed Monday morning. It's possible that you may be one of the eight out of ten people who are in the wrong type of employment. These statistics might appear high, but if you conduct your own survey, you'll likely confirm that it's true.

Ask people if they feel they're in the right job for them, or is there another job they'd rather be doing. Ask yourself that question too. If you said you're in the wrong job, you may have to find more suitable employment. After all, you likely spend about ten hours a day, five days a week getting ready for, travelling to, or working at your job. Isn't it worth the effort to find out what kind of job you'd be happy in? Or is it easier to stay in the rut?

Having control over your life is a necessity for lifelong happiness. Allow yourself that control and you'll allow yourself to have a happier, healthier and more positive life.

6. You use such phrases as "If only . . . or I should have . . . "

There are many cop-out phrases you may be using to bind yourself to the past. Do you find yourself using phrases such as:

> *"If only I were younger, slimmer, more attractive . . . "*
> *"I should have done this years ago."*
> *"I should have been more careful."*
> *"I was supposed to . . . "*
> *"I ought to . . . "*
> *"I have to . . . "*
> *"I must . . . "*
> *"I need to . . . "*
> *"I'm trying to . . . "*
> *"If you want me to . . . "*
> *"S/he made me . . . "*
> *"You always . . . "*
> *"You never . . . "*
> *"I'm this way because . . . "*
> *"I can't change the way I am because . . . "*
> *"The trouble with . . . "*
> *"I can't . . . "*

Whenever possible, eliminate these phrases from your vocabulary unless you're willing to do something constructive about your comments.

Using Logic

It's easy to respond to situations with emotions rather than logic but by responding logically, you can keep from over-reacting. Achieve this by analyzing situations to determine whether you're reacting correctly.

This won't come automatically. It takes hard, concentrated effort. Practice this skill until you automatically respond the way you want to. You may find yourself slipping back into your old defensive, or retaliatory ways, but keep at it. If you realize you're still stewing over something, and it's ten minutes after the negative situation, it's not too late to throw away the negative feelings. Remember *You choose to*:

* let others give you their anger
* let yourself become angry because someone put a dent in your car door or you got stuck in traffic
* feel guilty when you couldn't please others or because you made a mistake
* spend your valuable time on revengeful actions
* feel stressed when you face an overload of work
* feel depressed for no other reason than it's Monday morning
* live in the past using phrases such as *"If only . . . "* and *"I should have . . . "*

If you're feeling any of these negative feelings, stop and ask yourself these questions:

1. Am I reacting correctly in this situation?
2. Should I really be having these negative feelings?
3. Could I be over-reacting?

If any of these is the case, stop yourself and vow that you won't allow these negative feelings to affect the next few minutes, hours, days or weeks of your life!

How to reduce frustration and anger

We all feel angry and upset at times. This can occur when we have a need, and something (a barricade or block) keeps us from meeting that need. We're likely to start by feeling frustrated. The longer the block remains, the more frustrated we can become and eventually, the block can lead to anger. These two strong negative emotions can happen almost simultaneously.

FRUSTRATION AND ANGER

NEED	BLOCK	SATISFACTION OF NEED

Whenever you run into a situation where you can't get what you want, or see others who are frustrated, take time to

15

identify the "block." Then, determine how you can remove the block which will satisfy the need.

Handling Stress

Do you feel like moving to a desert island when your frustrations become overwhelming? If you find your life too stressful, the following exercise can help you get yourself back on track. It's especially helpful if you find you have more worries than you can handle, or if your frustration and anger levels are at the boiling point. Give yourself at least one or two hours to do this exercise properly. Write things down - don't just go through the mental process.

To accomplish this:

1. Write down all situations that cause you frustration, worry, or anger. These could be in your personal, business and social life. BE SPECIFIC!

2. Then determine whether:
   (a) You DO have the power to change the situation - can do something to remove the problem. Put the word DO next to the situation.
      For instance, *"I worry about my daughter. She's in daycare, and when I pick her up at night, all the children at the centre are fussy, crying and hard to handle."*
      You DO have the power to change this situation by putting her in another more suitable day care centre.
   (b) You DON'T have the power to change the situation. It's beyond your control - there's nothing you can do about the situation. Put the word DON'T next to the situation.
      For instance, *"I worry about my son. He's in grade two and I'm worried that he might get hurt at school by falling down the stairs or getting hit by a baseball."*
      You DON'T really have control over accidents he may have at school or when he's away from you.

      NOTE: Most of the "If only . . . " and "I should have . . . " situations fall into this category.

16

3. List those items you DON'T have the power to do something about, and commit them to memory. Then vow not to waste your precious energy and time thinking about the issues again. If you find yourself dwelling time after time on negative situations that happened in the past, or on situations you don't have the power to change - try this tactic. Place a loose elastic band around your wrist and snap it whenever you catch yourself, mulling over these thoughts. Soon, this painful reminder will enable you to re-channel your energy towards more positive ideas.
4. If you DO have the power to change the situation, what do you plan to do about it? (Or are you simply going to complain about the situation to others?)

Set some concrete, written goals about what you *can* do, and follow-through with your plan. Some situations may have to go on "hold" until the timing's right, but set some goals for when the timing *is* right.

These four steps put the Serenity Prayer (written by Reinhold Niebuhr) into action:

"GOD GRANT ME THE SERENITY TO ACCEPT THE THINGS I CANNOT CHANGE, THE COURAGE TO CHANGE THE THINGS I CAN, AND THE WISDOM TO KNOW THE DIFFERENCE."

I have a very busy and stressful life and find that sometimes, life starts closing in on me. I've found that the four-step process just identified works well for me. Completed once or twice a year (or whenever necessary) it reduces my stress level by half and sometimes more.

When I get to step two, I can normally throw out one-third of the problems I've been worrying about. I then concentrate my efforts on changing the situations I DO have control over, and channel my energy towards eliminating many of my worries, frustrations and anger.

The benefits of doing the above, are: I'll throw out many unnecessary worries, frustrations and anger, put some on "hold," and chart a course of action to help solve the remaining problems.

Criticism

You may respond negatively to others' criticism. How others criticize you decides whether a positive or negative reaction is the outcome. There are two basic ways to criticize. One is constructive and has positive results. The other is destructive and normally triggers the person's defense mechanism.

Destructive Criticism

This is where others criticize YOU as a person - not your behaviour. This criticism strikes at your inner core, and can often damage your feeling of self-worth. For example:

"Joan, stop clacking your gum! You're the most selfish person I know! You don't care anything about the people who have to live with you!"

If you were Joan, you'd probably react in a defensive way (because you probably felt that you were attacked). Your negative behaviour would likely continue.

Constructive Criticism

Constructive criticism tries to correct your behaviour. This form of constructive criticism concentrates on your offensive behaviour, identifies the offended person's feelings, and gives you a chance to correct your behaviour. For example:

"Joan, I'm finding that your gum cracking is distracting me from reading my book. Would you like this roll of peppermints instead?"

The behaviour they're correcting is - You're cracking your gum. You're not likely to continue the behaviour in the future. Keep this in mind when correcting others' behaviour. Concentrate on their behaviour, not on labelling them as a person. (More on this topic in Chapter 8).

If you're the receiver of criticism (whether it's constructive or destructive) you may still feel like responding defensively. Before allowing your defense mechanism to kick in consider the following:

1. Control your thoughts and behaviour. Keep in mind there MAY be some truth to the criticism.

2. If the criticism is valid - apologize. Let the person know what steps you'll take to correct the behaviour or problem. Strive not to repeat this failure or cause the problem in the future. Leave feelings of guilt behind. Don't let the criticism over-whelm you and affect the rest of your day. Instead, learn from your mistakes.
3. When others criticize you, don't immediately feel you must retaliate. Instead, listen carefully to their comments.
4. Ask for specifics if the criticism is vague. For instance, the person says, *"I don't like your attitude."* This is very vague, so ask the person for specifics. (Watch your tone of voice).

   Don't make your comments accusatory, otherwise the person will become defensive). *"What is it about my attitude that concerns you?"*

   "Well, you made some nasty comments to Pat when she was visiting us. I know you don't agree with everything she says, but I feel you should be courteous to her because she's my friend."

   Now you have something specific you can discuss.
5. Confirm your understanding of the problem (using para-phrasing - see Chapter 3).
6. Don't climb into a shell when others criticize you for something. We often set up this kind of defense mechanism in ourselves. If something or someone hurts us (especially someone we're close to) we're likely to withdraw and "lick our wounds." This can double the negative effects of the problem.

NO isn't a dirty word

Do you find yourself in trouble when others ask you to do something for them? Do you want to say "No," but end up saying "Yes" instead? Is it possible that you say "Yes" for any of the following reasons?

* You don't want to hurt someone's feelings?
* You don't want to explain why you want to say no?
* You don't want to say anything the other person might interpret as negative?
* You feel compelled to spend time with the person because you haven't seen her or him in months?

19

* The other person is particularly important to you?
* You would really like to oblige, but the timing is inappropriate.

Learning how to say "No" when you want to, depends on increasing:

* Your self-respect.
* Your confidence about following your standards and decisions.
* Your comfort about meeting your personal needs.
* Your recognition that you aren't responsible for others' feelings.
* Your understanding that your worth does not depend on other people's judgements.
* Your comfort and confidence in pleasing yourself.
* Understanding that you can't please all the people, all the time.

If you have trouble saying "No" to requests. Each step forward can help you learn when and how to say "No" comfortably and effectively. Try the following:

Step 1: Identify a situation where you said "Yes" inappropriately.

Step 2: Identify the reasons why you said "Yes." Were you concerned that you had to say "Yes" otherwise you might injure the relationship? Were you worried about the other person's feelings?

Step 3: Prepare yourself for the next occasion that will prevent the situation from happening again.

Step 4: Practice your new response. Rehearsing with an uninvolved person might help you have the confidence you need to carry your plan to completion.

NOTE: Always know what *you* want, before you decide to say "Yes." Don't allow yourself to feel compelled to return a favour from a friend. Stop saying "Yes" to people because you believe "No" will hurt their feelings.

CHAPTER 2
MALE-FEMALE COMMUNICATION STYLES

Misunderstood Communication Messages

Unfortunately, the simple act of communicating with one another, can cause confused or missed messages. This is especially true with communication between men and women. It's no wonder there's conflict, when men and women interpret the same conversation in such different ways. This is because of the different conversational styles of men and women.

Many examples given in this chapter will stereotype male/female responses. There are many exceptions to the examples I've identified. Analyze how you feel or respond to situations. Compare them to those described, and decide if you need to change anything in your communication to enhance compatibility.

As women grow up, talk is the thread with which they weave relationships. They develop and maintain friendships by exchanging secrets, and regard talking as the cornerstone of friendships with both men and women.

When women get together, they talk about personal matters - situations that happen at home and at work. Men are more likely to talk about sports, politics and other topics, but stay clear of talking about their personal life. In female to male communication, the woman asks most of the questions. Women see questions as a way to continue a conversation, while men view questions as requests for information.

When a woman marries, she expects her husband to be her best friend. Men don't know what kind of talk women want, and don't miss it when it isn't there. Men, therefore, are less likely to ask personal questions. They believe that if she wants to tell him something, she'll tell him. Men often think questions show intrusion, while women believe they express interest and intimacy.

Boys bond as intensely as girls, but base their friendships more on doing activities together and don't require talk to cement relationships. Men converse to establish their status - women to create rapport with others. Men are comfortable telling people what to do. Women don't like to pull rank, so request, rather than demand. Therefore, men often believe they have the right to accept or refuse the woman's request.

For example: A female supervisor wanted Mark to help Joe get a job done, so said, *"Joe looks as if he could use your help."*

Mark replied, *"You're right he does seem to need help."*

Later, the supervisor became upset when she found Joe still struggling along, and learned that Mark had not offered to help. Mark thought that she was just making conversation, not asking him to help Joe. Because he had other, more pressing tasks to do, he hadn't thought her comment was important.

The supervisor should have been clearer in her communication with Mark. She had supervised women in the past, and that was the style of management that worked best with them. She didn't understand that men required a different kind of direction from her. She should have stated, *"Mark, Joe needs help so I want you to leave the Miller report and help him until he completes his assignment."* Mark would then know that she had prioritized Joe's project over the one he was working on, so he would have immediately helped Joe.

On the other hand, if she's seen as too authoritarian, she's often labelled "aggressive." Unfortunately when women don't try to please others, their behaviour results in the belief by colleagues, supervisors and friends that she's too aggressive. This fine line is hard to define. Women will continue teetering on the edge, until there are more women capable of speaking their minds without compromising their basic natures.

Women face each other directly with eyes anchored on each others' faces when conversing. Boys and men sit at angles to each other and look elsewhere in the room -periodically glancing at each other. They often mirror each other's body movements. Men's tendency to face away from them when conversing, gives women the impression that the men aren't listening to them, when in fact they are. The only times men will really look at a speaker for any length of time are;

a) if they're trying to evaluate whether the speaker is lying or not,
b) the speaker is hostile and they may be forced to take defensive action, or
c) they're evaluating an attractive woman.

In the latter, they'll glance over the woman's body while listening to her comments. This is highly distracting to the female speaker because his eyes mirror that he's not really listening to what she's saying, but rather sizing her up as a woman.

Another habit that gives women the impression men aren't listening is that they switch topics more often. Women talk at length about one topic - men jump from topic to topic.

When a woman expresses her point of view, her female listeners usually express agreement and support. Women prefer other points of view expressed as suggestions and inquiries rather than as direct challenges or arguments.

Men point out the other side of the issue. Women see this as disloyalty and a refusal to offer support for their ideas. Men are more comfortable with an oppositional approach. A discussion becomes a debate and a conversation can become a competitive sport. Men are more likely to stick to facts and opinions. This comes across to women as authoritarian, not comprehending that it illustrates the masculine form of communicating rather than a show of supremacy.

Women use the pronouns "you" and "we" much more than men and use conversational connections such as *"Yes, but . . . "* to acknowledge a previous comment. Because men don't normally use this - they often ignore the woman's comments.

Women (and some men) often phrase their comments to sound as if they are questions. *"Our meeting is at . . . three?"* This rising inflection at the end of a sentence is an implied question and leaves the listener with the impression that she's uncertain of what she's saying.

For example: A woman at a community club board meeting said, *"Ummm, I'd like to say something. This may sound dumb - it's just a thought - but maybe before we discuss program strategies, we should figure out our goals. I mean, I don't know what you think, but it sounds logical to me . . . "*
The men on the committee ignored her comments. At their next meeting, a male member brought up the same issue, which was promptly accepted and discussed at length. The woman's tentative, uncertain style made the men in the group think her ideas weren't listening to, when in fact they were. She lacked power in her style of communication. Her traditional training said that she should constantly try to please others, and should appear as if she agreed with others' values and opinions.

Other timid speakers start sentences with, *"I probably shouldn't say anything but . . . "* Or, *"I don't know what you feel about this . . . "* Or, *"One suggestion I'd like to make . . . "* and, *"I just wanted to know if . . . "* which all show weakness.

Listening noises

Men expect silent attention from their listener, and interpret a stream of listener noise as overreaction or impatience by their female listener. When women talk to each other, they often overlap, finish each other's sentences and anticipate what the other is about to say. If women do this while conversing with men, they may view this as an interruption, feel she's being rude, and could be displaying a lack of attention to what they've been talking about.

Women make more listening noises like, *"uh-huh . . . "* to encourage the other person. Men believe these noises mean the woman agrees with him, when she may not agree with him at all.

Because men don't make as many listening noises, women assume they're not really listening.   Men are less likely to make non-verbal signs of listening either, and many continue doing whatever they were doing before the conversation began. Women are more likely to nod their head more, give direct eye contact, and stop whatever else they may have been doing when the conversation began.

Use of Humour

Often the widest division between who's in on the joke and who's left out, is between men and women.   They don't necessarily find the same situations funny.   Women often wonder why men don't think their jokes are funny, and other times wonder what men are laughing at.

Young boys get more pleasure in hostile humour than girls.   At an early age, boys choose aggressive cartoons as the funnier ones.   Even at the age of three, boys are more likely to act silly, make faces and horse around than girls.   They practice this on each other from childhood.

Women are more likely to joke about the powerful, not the pitiful, concentrate on big issues and question the way the world is put together.   They traditionally used self-depreciating humour even if it erodes their self-esteem.   It's not threatening for a woman to joke, if she's only joking about herself or other women.   However, if she tells a joke about the male power aristocracy in front of a member of that group, the man may feel threatened and angry.

Female humour shows a refusal to take authority seriously and are less likely to look up to supervisors than men.   Women's humour directs some of its most effective material at men, questioning their authority and showing a certain amount of disdain.   Women see the "rules of the game" in business as mainly childish games that only the "boys" would consider playing.   In this way, women's comedy can be more ominous than men's.

Women are more likely to console, rather than laugh at anyone considered a "victim."   This is one of the reasons certain forms of slapstick comedy appeal far less to women than to men.   Men are more prone to use slapstick comedy (such as the

Three Stooges poking each other in the eye) that many women do not find the least bit funny.

Women are more likely to conjure up an image that is well known to others such as, *"Remember how Tim Allen on the Home Improvement Show did . . . "* Her communication says, *"I have an image in my mind. Do you have the same picture?"*

Men's humour also pokes fun at social conventions; and some accuse women of not laughing at a good joke. Often what the women are hearing is not funny, but rather hostility and sarcasm disguised as humour. When it comes to humour, men give, and women receive most of the time.

Men's humour often relates to the sexuality or sexual parts of the opposite sex. These include obscene or hostile jokes (with an intention of aggressiveness, satire or defense,) cynical jokes (critical and blasphemous) and sceptical jokes. These jokes mention forbidden subjects, engage in offensive or childish behaviour, slip beyond bounds of good taste, and often violate moral taboos. This type of joking has hostile elements (similar to the rough-and-tumble horseplay and shoving of young boys) that they use to vent aggression.

In this way, men's comedy feels more personal and insidious to women, who see the verbal blows as "below the belt" and not fair.

Confused messages

Here's a home situation that shows what often happens during communication between spouses. A couple has just returned from vacation and the wife is struggling to catch up with the family laundry, shopping and cleaning:

1. *Husband's Intention:* He wants to let his wife know that he recognizes and appreciates the extra load she's been carrying. He considers what he might do, to communicate how much he appreciates her working so hard:
   (a) Buy her some flowers.
   (b) Take her to dinner.
   (c) Tell her how he feels.
   (d) Be more helpful at home.

2. *Husband's Action:* He decides (d), and puts a load of laundry in the washer.
3. *Wife's Reaction:* She sees him doing the laundry, doesn't realize his intentions and has to decide:
   (a) Is he criticizing her for not having the table set?
   (b) Is he trying to tell her she shouldn't spend so much time on the phone?
   (c) Is he trying to be helpful?
   (d) Does he feel guilty about something?
4. *Affect on Wife:* She decides it's (a) and feels hurt and put down.
5. *Wife Encodes:* I'm not going to let him know that his actions have hurt me. Shall I:
   (a) Say nothing.
   (b) Say "Thanks."
6. *Wife's Action:* She decides to say "Thanks."
7. *Affect on Husband:* She understands and appreciates what I've done.

This is a classic situation where the husband's intention was positive and caring. However, the effect on his wife was the direct opposite of his intention. How much better it would have been if he had backed his actions up with words as shown in (c) husband's intentions. Using positive verbal feedback, he would have made sure his wife knew why he was helping her.

Power

The emotional roles men and women play out during arguments relate to the degree of power they feel within a relationship. Because women often find themselves in a subordinate role, they fall into the habit of restraining anger or expressing it in passive ways (such as whining, nagging or crying). Self-disclosure and discussing feelings are more comfortable for women. If these are not forthcoming from men, they feel threatened.

Men believe the games of business, politics and power are no different. Trying to beat another person and championing one's own view as hard as one can, doesn't mean you're hurting anyone else personally - it's just playing the game.

27

In marriage, when friction arises, many women believe that the marriage is working fine as long as they can discuss their problems (which she feels builds intimacy). The men feel that the marriage isn't working if they're constantly having to talk about it (he'd rather find a swift solution and go on to something else).

Excellent books on this topic are, *"You Just Don't Understand: Women and Men in Conversation"* by Deborah Tannen and *"The Incompatibility of Men and Women and How to Overcome It."* by Julius Fast.

Interruptions

Men are more likely to interrupt with negative side comments. On the other hand, women are more prone to finish each others' sentences and are very comfortable with this. Men clam up or react defensively when women do this with them, because they feel the woman's trying to take over the conversation.

Friendship

There seems to be a vast difference in the kinds of friendships that occur between men and those that occur between women. These differences are:

Female friendships

Female friendships usually involve talking about feelings and personal lives.

Back in the '50s women called their best female friends, their girlfriends. After they disbursed their husbands and children in the morning, these girlfriends gathered at one home or another. They drank coffee, gossiped, shared recipes and secrets, cared for and relied on each another. This ceased the minute their husbands appeared on the scene. The man of the family won out over girlfriends.

Today women meet under different circumstances, in conference rooms and restaurants. There's less time for every-day exchanges, and the topics are different. Instead of discussing recipes, they're more likely to discuss some professional crisis they're facing and the most recent fast-food ideas they can use to prepare dinner.

What's changed this attitude in women? Because children often move far away from their childhood support groups of siblings and parents, they find themselves facing problems their parents have never experienced. Problems, such as:

* how a woman can climb the corporate ladder
* what she should wear to look successful
* should she consider a common-law relationship
* what about birth control and abortion
* how to handle two-income family problems
* how to balance work and home responsibilities,

are all faced by modern women in the workforce. This is where other female friends provide their opinion and expertise.

The experiences of the two generations have become so different in such a short time, that women can't discuss their problems with their parents. If women really want to talk openly, they need knowledgeable contemporaries.

Factors that can have a negative affect on friendships, such as getting married, having a baby, or getting divorced, are more easily overcome when they have established strong bonds beforehand. Women meet some of their closest friends at work and maintain these friendships long after they've moved to different companies. Because of their limited time, when women get together, they get right down to nitty-gritty issues. There isn't enough time for chit chat, and conversations seem to deal with deep and meaningful topics.

Male friendships

Men have had access to a system of friendships that women call the "old boys' network" for centuries. They met in taverns, exclusive professional and social clubs (no women allowed). Men seldom worked in teams or networked with women. Men in the "baby-boomer" era are less authoritarian, and more team-oriented toward women than older men in the workplace.

Male friendships used to revolve around activities. Within the past generation this has all changed. Do men benefit as well as woman from the new emphasis on friendships out of the family or all-male circle? Yes, mainly because it's now acceptable for them to have close female friends. The biggest change in friendships, is that men and women have learned how to have solid, long-lasting platonic friendships.

Unfortunately, only one-third of men (compared to three-quarters of women) say they have a best friend. When they do, it's usually friendship with a woman. Both men and women may suffer through crisis alone, if a strong network of friends and supporters is not available. Both need a strong support group to handle the rigors of daily life.

Sharing thoughts and feelings

Most women are comfortable admitting negative feelings, but society has almost forbidden men to admit to these perceived weaknesses. Therefore, this limits their options for expressing their feelings. Many respond as if they're angry. This is an acceptable reaction among men. In reality, underneath this facade of being angry, they may feel hurt, defenceless or afraid, but still respond as if they're angry.

This ambiguous behaviour confuses women and adds to the male/female communication gap. On the other hand, when some women get angry, they end in tears. This gives men the impression that they're feeling sad or hurt, which adds to their confusion.

Often, women turn to their female friends for emotional support. The turnaround is that these friendships (at times) can often be stronger and longer-lasting than those they share with their husbands. They're finding their friendships with other women to be the most intimate, profound, and durable relationships of their lives. For many women, these ties are also stronger than their family ties. Women no longer use friends as stand-ins for family; instead, friends are becoming part of an extended family. Unexpectedly, these friendships result in stronger marriages, because spouses are no longer expected to meet their wives' emotional needs exclusively.

Many women complain that the men in their lives don't share their thoughts and feelings with them - that it's the most important communication problem in their relationships with men. They feel that their men don't trust them, so shut them out from learning what their feelings are. This male vulnerability keeps many men and women from sharing true intimacy.

As one woman put it, *"My friend Sally and I go way back to childhood. I can tell her anything and we share all our feelings. I'll never have that kind of intimacy with the men in my life because they just won't let me get close enough to understand their true emotions. They won't share their deepest feelings with me.*

When I see my husband is distressed about something and ask what's wrong - he shrugs me off with, 'I don't want to talk about it. ' When he does this, I feel shut out by him, but nothing I say can convince him how I feel. He accuses me of being too sensitive. I've come to the conclusion that nothing I do, will overcome the lifelong conditioning that taught him to mask his negative feelings. The last thing he seems able to do, is talk to me about it. "

Through the centuries, men were the protectors of the home. Society expected them to keep emotionally detached and separate, by suppressing their compassion and softer emotions. It expected men to tolerate hardship and pain so they could function fully. Society said they were allowed to show happiness and anger but were not allowed to show any feelings between those two emotions. Therefore, when men felt anxious, disappointed, jealous, sad, hurt, rejected, stupid, intimidated, insecure, ashamed, or ignored, their outward appearance would show the misleading verbal and non-verbal signs of anger.

Some men have taken the chance, have confided their innermost feelings to their wives, and have been betrayed. As Mike explained, *"I let down the barriers a couple of times with my wife and gave her confidential information. She didn't keep that information to herself, so I can't trust her any more. "* His feelings are understandable, and women should be very careful not to betray their husbands' confidences.

When men feel upset about something, most of them need time and privacy to mull over the situation. They see their wives' insistence on sharing the problem as interference to this process. If their wives persist, they believe she's nagging, and pull further into themselves. This interference by their wives into their efforts to solve their original problem, leads to even more frustration.

Both partners need to be flexible and empathize with what's going on with the other person, and understand what's behind the other person's behaviour. The only way this will occur, is if they discuss their feelings and ask for the other's co-operation.

The wife should back off, letting her husband know that she's there when he's ready to talk about his problem. Instead of giving into his initial desire to push her away from him, he should try to understand that she needs to "make everything right." Her nurturing nature makes her want to help, not invade his space. To make this effective, he needs to examine what he's *really* feeling at the time, and put those feelings into words. For this process to work, men require enormous trust in their partners before feeling free to reveal their vulnerable inner selves.

What the wife should not tolerate, are spin-off negative behaviours that might accompany the man's distress. If he's lashing out at others, throwing things, or displaying his negative feelings in destructive ways, his wife has every right to interfere.

She could use this approach, *"I can see you're distressed about something and understand that you don't want to talk to me about it now, but I can't stand by and condone your destructive behaviour. We have to talk about this because of the spin-off problems it's causing, not only for me, but for our children. "* The man would do the same if it was the woman who was bottling up her anger or releasing it by throwing items.

Intimacy

Intimacy involves having complete trust in another person. You obtain intimacy by "letting it all hang out" and allowing others to know what's happening inside you. The ability of allowing people to see the "real you" may be overshadowed by the fear that others may use this weapon against you in the future.

Intimacy involves revealing how you *really* feel about what the other person does and considers the other person's feelings when communicating with them. This involves a considerable amount of empathy. The benefits of revealing your true self, are that the other person can almost know how you'll react to situations, and will try to stay clear of those that will upset you. They'll automatically protect you from situations that might unnerve or upset you, and find ways around difficult situations so you won't feel hurt.

When we look at marital relationships that survive, we find that the couple are good friends and treat each other with respect. They have shared values and trust each other. Trust is the foundation of the relationship and without it, neither will feel safe. Unless they establish this trust, true intimacy will not occur. If they don't feel safe, they can't be vulnerable. If they're not vulnerable, they can't be intimate.

If you observe people getting to know each other (of the same or mixed genders), there are several steps they take to get to the stage where they reach intimacy.

* One person reveals trusting information. The second person accepts that trust and reveals similar information.
* As the trust grows between these people, they enlarge their trust and reveal more and more. This could be almost instantaneous, or could take months to occur, depending on the comfort zone of the participants.

This feeling of intimacy could end suddenly should one person do something that the other sees as a betrayal of their trust. Betrayal doesn't necessarily have to be verbal. It could be that they said they'd do something, and didn't follow through. It could be that they were late for an important function, didn't do something they said they would do, or anything else that could shake the trust in either participant. If loss of trust occurs in a deep friendship or relationship - the participants must talk about it. The person who feels betrayed would share his or her misgivings with the offending person.

When a couple "snipe" at each other, they lose trust in each other. Studies still show that the ultimate betrayal between couples is infidelity.

A good book on this topic is, *"The Intimacy Struggle,"* by Dr. Janet Woititz.

Love & Sex

Don and Irene's marriage was in trouble. As Irene explained, *"All my husband wants is SEX. I just wish that for once, there would be some romance and love during our intimate moments."*

In marriage, women use talk to create intimacy, where they openly express their feelings and thoughts. Men use touch and actions (bringing her flowers, rubbing her back, doing nice things for her) to create intimacy (using non-verbal communication) and talk to maintain independence. They're on guard to protect themselves from put-downs or others who might want to push them around. If they give others (even their wives) the weaponry (talk about their weaknesses) it could be used against them in the future - so they clam up and resist verbal intimacy.

Studies show that men want more sex; women want more love. Both are behaving in their own way without understanding the meaning behind the other's behaviour. Surveys indicate that most men think about sex about six times in an hour (and also during their fantasies when sleeping). Unless they're stimulated by some external force, most women seldom think about the sex act, except to think about the romance surrounding it.

Because women were physically weaker, men traditionally were responsible for protecting their women and children. This put them in charge. Women's traditional duty was to offer their bodies to men for procreation. In return men would protect the women and their offspring. If men failed in this endeavour, society believed they were weak and ineffectual. This discouraged men from loving the women who wanted it so desperately, mainly because of their training on how *not* to give it to others. Their version of love was (and often still is) through sex, the primary way they express and accept intimacy. To this day, men seldom know how to meet women's needs, let alone how to get them to meet their own need for physical sex.

On the other hand, women want love and closeness, and want to offer love and nurturing, but the sexual nature of men's attentions turn them off. They often feel that men don't love them, but just use them for sex. Women want to connect with men emotionally through lovemaking especially *before* having sex. They want a deep relationship with men who not only understand their needs, but accept them for who they are. They want to know how men *really* feel, but many find men incapable of understanding or verbalizing how they really feel.

So what's the answer? A woman needs to give her man feedback, explaining how she really feels. If necessary, she may have to give explicit instructions on what she requires him to do, so she can feel loved and wanted and so she's not seen primarily as a sexual object. In turn, women must feel comfortable with their own sexuality and let their men know they DO enjoy sex if they're properly prepared for it.

Men need to unlearn their initial training by gaining knowledge of how to turn a woman on. A man can accomplish this by giving her the love she needs and wants, before attempting sexual intercourse. He still needs to make the woman feel that she's safe, that he isn't using her, and that he cares deeply for her. Both men and women need to meet half way; she to secure the love she wants, and he to get the sex he wants.

Male/Female Reactions to Situations

Men and women have problems communicating in everyday, mundane situations. Male and female approaches to situations differ in so many ways. These differences can accumulate until the couple wonder if they think and act alike under ANY circumstances. See if you recognize any of the following:

Situation #1
"We're lost." exclaimed the wife, *"Let's stop and ask someone for directions."*

Husband, *"Give me that map! I shouldn't have relied on you for directions!"*

Then he spends the next half hour trying to learn where they are, in relation to where they wanted to go. Why won't he ask someone else for directions? He explained that he doesn't want anyone to know he's in trouble - he'd rather find his way out by himself. This way no one can get "one up on him."

Normally, women feel very comfortable asking others for direction and help. They can't understand the stubbornness of their partner in this kind of situation.

Situation #2
A married couple were shopping in a mall. The wife was hungry, so she asked her husband, *"Would you like to stop and have some lunch?"*

He answered, *"No, I'm not hungry yet and we've still got a lot of shopping to do."* So they didn't stop for lunch.

The result was, the wife became annoyed with him because she felt that he didn't consider her wishes. Unfortunately, the husband didn't see that his wife had wanted to stop to fulfil her own needs. She should have been more direct and said, *"I'm hungry. Let's stop for something to eat."*

Women use talking as a way of giving support and nurturing. Men use conversation to either achieve the upper hand or to prevent other people from pushing them around. She should have stated clearly what she wanted from him.

Situation #3
A wife explained her frustration at her inability to lose weight. She became upset when her husband listed five solutions to her problem.

A woman may discuss a problem she's had during her day with her husband. She expects to receive a sympathetic ear, and listening noises such as, *"I see . . ., uhm hm . . . "* Instead, the man believes she's identified a problem so he can help her solve it. Because he believes this, he makes several suggestions about how she can solve her problem. The woman feels he's showing her that she can't handle the problem herself and feels hurt.

When women have a complaint, they often look for emotional support (not solutions). When men hear a complaint, they feel challenged to come up with a solution.

What he should have said was, *"Do you want my help with this problem?"* before diving in with solutions. The man's intentions were good. Male communication dictates that when someone identifies a problem to them, they should give solutions - not sympathy.

Situation #4
A husband complained that he didn't feel like getting out of bed; that he ached all over and he didn't feel very well. His wife stroked his brow and gave him sympathy. He became upset

because she didn't seem to be interested in making him feel better. She gave emotional support, he wanted solutions.

Situation #5
Women say, *"I think it's about time we saw a movie."* Or, *"This weekend, we should clean the basement."*

He interprets these kinds of comments as commands, resists her telling him what to do, feels manipulated, so responds resentfully. She thinks she's making suggestions, and presents her requests as ideas, not demands. He would respond much better if she had made straightforward requests - not suggestions. *"I want to go to a movie tonight. What do you want to do?"* Or *"The basement is a real mess. What do you say we clean it this weekend?"*

Situation #6
A wife spent a considerable time explaining to her husband about her day. Nothing of any significance happened, and her husband stated, *"What's your point?"*

The wife felt devastated that her husband thought what she did all day was insignificant. He on the other hand, wondered where she was going with her comments, and waited for the punch line (which never came). He felt disappointed because she wasted his time by talking about unimportant issues.

Women's interest focuses on interrelationships, men's on the significance of the information given.

Situation #7
At a recent seminar with both of men and women, I noticed that one man had been very talkative, while his wife sat silently beside him. Toward the end of the evening, I mentioned that women frequently complain that their husbands don't talk to them. The man agreed with my comment and stated *"She's the talker in our family."* The audience burst out laughing, while the man looked puzzled and hurt.

"It's true," he illuminated. *"When I come home from work, I have nothing to say. If she didn't keep the conversation going, we'd spend the whole evening in silence."*

This situation points out the incongruity of the usual conversational styles of men and women. Men talk more than women in public situations, and often talk less at home. This pattern has caused havoc in marriages. The solution is for both men and women to adjust and bridge the gap between their diverse conversational styles. Women can often meet their socializing needs by talking with other women.

Situation #8
Most arguments between couples start when a woman tries to start a discussion about a problem they face together. The man, (at least at first), will likely try to avoid it. Once the dispute gets under way however, men want to come up with a solution FAST. Women want to discuss the problem, its possible solutions and ramifications, before coming to a decision.

Women are more likely to see a conflict as stemming from within the relationship; men see conflict as coming from something outside it. Most conflicts are about trust, power or intimacy. Women complain that their men withdraw from conflicts, and don't share enough. Men and women who respond to conflicts defensively, stubbornly, or who consistently withdraw, may do the most damage to their own and their partner's happiness. Those couples who never fight because they're afraid to rock the boat, may be unhappier in the end, than those who DO fight.

Resolving Conflicts

Men complain that women nag and are too emotional. In men, stressful situations trigger a fast rise in his heart rate and blood pressure (fight or flight response). When he feels that surge in blood pressure at the anticipation of an argument, his body and brain react in self-preservation. Women's nurturing peace-keeping nature is more likely to choose a way through the conflict using compromise or negotiation.

Only when both men and women give consistent effort toward understanding why the other gender does what it does, can they communicate on the same "wave length." This takes patience, empathy and a degree of openness that may be uncomfortable for men. Women need to be patient while men learn to trust them during the process of overcoming centuries of programming that tells them they should keep their feelings to themselves.

CHAPTER 3
COMMUNICATION SKILLS FOR
DEALING WITH DIFFICULT PEOPLE

Communication Process

If you find there are too many situations where either you misunderstand others or they misinterpret your messages, you'll have to work on your communication skills. There are eight steps in the communication process between two people:

COMMUNICATION PROCESS

1. What I want to say.
2. What I actually say.
3. What the other person hears.
4. What the person thinks s/he hears.
5. How the person wants to respond.
6. How the person actually responds.
7. What I hear the person say.
8. What I think I hear the person say.

Same Words - Different meanings

Often words mean different things to different people. For example, if I invited you to my place for dinner tomorrow, when would you come? Would it be at noon, 1:00, 5:00, 6:00, 7:00, or 8:00 p.m.? Some people have *dinner* (the main meal of the day) at noon, others in the evening.

If I asked people from Alaska and Florida to describe a blizzard, do you think their descriptions would be the same? Of course not - because each person comes with a pre-conceived notion of what this word means to them. And if you asked a teenager what a blizzard was, they'd probably say that it's an ice cream treat that you eat!

In North America we'd say, *"Just a minute."* In Ireland they'd say, *"Hang on two ticks."* In North America you'd refer to the people who work with you as, "co-workers." In Australia and Great Britain they'd use the expression, "workmates." In Scotland, an often heard expression is *"I dinna ken."* Which means *"I don't understand."* In England, an expression that brings smiles to faces of North Americans is, *"I'll knock you up in the morning."* Which means *"I'll wake you in the morning."*

English is one of the hardest languages to learn. When you consider these double-meaning words, I'm sure you'll agree:

razed (demolished)	raised (elevated)
picture (illustration)	pitcher (urn)
read (comprehend)	red (colour)
witch (crone)	which (what one)
lead (pencil)	lead (to precede)
lie (untruth)	lye (alkaline solution)

Meanings of words - male/female

Often the same word has different meanings to men and women. I was with a group of people socially, when a young woman in the group was discussing her career aspirations. She had attended a job interview that morning. Her boyfriend asked her whether she'd accept the job if the company offered it to her.

She replied, *"Well, it would be a real challenge."*

Her male friend then stated, "Then, I guess you'd turn it down."

She said, *"Oh no, I'd take it if they offer it to me!"*

"But why would you - when it'll be such a difficult position?" he repeated.

She, *"I'd jump at the chance to get this position. As I explained, this job will be a real challenge for me!"*

The conversation progressed until it turned into a heated argument. The rest of us sat by, wondering what they were arguing about. It suddenly became apparent that they had entirely different definitions of the word "challenge." To clarify matters, we asked them to explain what the word meant to each of them.

The word "challenge" had a positive meaning for her. The women explained that the word challenge meant:
* The position would allow her to grow and stretch, to reach her full potential.
* That something was exciting.
* The job would give her a chance to prove herself.

Her male companion on the other hand, believed the word "challenge" had a negative meaning to it, and that it meant:
* That someone or something was standing in his way, keeping him from getting what he wanted.
* That he'd have a fight on his hands and he'd have to defend himself.

This revelation started the group trying to identify words they felt had different meanings to men and women. We decided that the following words have different meanings:

Macho - to most men it meant:
* a strong, decisive, leader that others respect,
* a trend setter, and role model.
   - to most women (and some men) it meant:
* a chauvinistic man who thinks he's "God's gift to women,"
* small or narrow minded,
* Atlas (pictured him kicking sand at weaker people),
* never passes a mirror without stopping to check his appearance and posture.

Gentle (when used to describe a man) - to most women it meant:
* tender, empathetic, in tune with others,

41

* doesn't take advantage of others,
* dependable, unassuming, trustworthy, kind-hearted
  - to most men it meant:
* mentally weak, soft, wishy-washy - they picture a wimp,
* indecisive, others can push them around,
* uses passive behaviour,
* is physically weak.

There are thousands of words we use in our every-day life that have these double meanings to men and women. I'm sure you know many others.

The next skill will make sure that what others' have said, is really what you heard them say.

Skill of Paraphrasing

This skill deals with the use of words. Paraphrasing means:
* To express meaning in other words.
* A restatement of text or work.
* Giving the meaning another form.
* Amplifying a message.

We normally use paraphrasing for simple comments such as, repeating telephone numbers when taking a message. But, how often do we transpose two numbers when taking down the seven simple digits of a phone number? The use of paraphrasing is essential whenever two people are conversing. Unfortunately, when information isn't clear, we often make assumptions. We don't confirm with the other person that what we *thought* they said, was what they really meant us to understand.

Has anyone ever given you instructions on how to get to their home and you neglected to use paraphrasing? Did you forget to make sure you understood their directions, and ended up in a phone booth asking for more directions?

When using paraphrasing, we often start sentences with:
"Do you mean that . . . ?"
"I want to make sure I understood (was clear about) what you said . . . "
"You say you felt upset when I . . . "
"You want me to . . . "

Here's an example of two people talking but not understanding each other:

42

Bob: *"Jim didn't get the job he applied for."*

Jennie: *"You mean, he didn't get the job he applied for?"*

Bob: *"Yeah, and he's really upset about it."*

In this conversation, Jennie thought she was using paraphrasing, but all she was doing was parroting what Bob said. Instead, she should have asked herself what Bob's statement *meant* to her. Some of her assumptions could have been:

- Jim may have asked for too high a salary.
- He was overqualified for the position.
- He was underqualified for the position.
- He blew the interview.
- There was a better candidate.
- He's probably better suited to a different career.

After determining what the statement meant to her, (which in this case was that Jim blew the interview), she used paraphrasing. The resulting conversation would then have been more like:

Bob: *"Jim didn't get that job he wanted."*

Jennie: *"You mean he blew the interview?"*

Bob: *"Oh no, he learned that they had already chosen someone else for the position before he applied."*

Jennie: *"That's too bad. I know he really wanted that job."*

Bob: *"Yeah, and he's really upset about it."*

You can see the differences between these two sets of conversations. In the first conversation, Bob and Jennie did not confirm their personal beliefs to one another. For instance, hat Jennie *knows* that Jim didn't get the job, because the company chose someone else for the position. Jennie on the other hand, believes that Bob has confirmed her belief that Jim blew the interview.

This is why problems occurred later. In a conversation with another friend, Jennie stated both she and Bob agreed that Jim had blown the interview. She honestly believed that she was speaking the truth to her friend.

This kind of problem exists in most conversations. Ask for more information if you're not sure what a person means, or use paraphrasing to bring out discrepancies. You probably use this technique already, but haven't been aware of it. If anyone has ever exclaimed, *"No that's not what I meant"* - you've already used paraphrasing. Use it often to lessen communication problems.

Use of Paraphrasing when instructing:

If you've had the responsibility of teaching new tasks to family members or friends, you've probably thrown your hands in the air at times because you had to explain how to do something repeatedly. Your information seems to go in one ear and out the other with some learners. Many people require constant repetition of instructions. This type of person could be a poor listener.

Paraphrasing is a very effective tool to use when training others, especially if they're lazy listeners. To help them retain the information and use it effectively, do the following:

1. Give them short, sequential instructions.

2. State, "To make sure that I was clear in my instructions to you, could you please explain what you're going to do?"

3. If they give you a blank look, and are unable to relate the steps;

4. Repeat the short, sequential instructions.

5. Again ask them to relate the steps they will take to complete the task.

You'll find that their listening skills will improve. They'll know that when you teach them to do anything new, there'll be a TEST to see if they've listened properly. Give the learner written back-up information for future reference. Whenever possible, demonstrate how they should complete the assignment. You'll find that instruction-giving will be much easier in the future.

Retention of information

The following method teaches learners how to be better listeners. Keep in mind that most people retain:

> **10%** of what they read (written information).
> **20%** of what they hear (have explained to them).
> **30%** of what they see done (demonstrations).
> **50%** of what they read, hear, and see done.
> **70%** of what they read, hear, see done, then they explain what they'll do (paraphrase).
> **90%** of what they read, hear, see done, they explain what they'll do, then demonstrate the task themselves.

You'll notice that your learner uses paraphrasing to confirm that s/he has understood your instructions. Do, however, remember that the onus is on you to make your instructions clear. Using such questions as:

"Do you understand?" (Doesn't confirm that they DID understand what you asked them to do.)

"Repeat what I told you to do." (This will just get their backs up).

"Did you catch that?" (A put-down because you're insinuating they aren't bright enough to pick up the information).

If they misunderstand you, it's much better to make the problem yours. You can accomplish this by such statements as:

"So I'm sure I was clear in my information . . . "

"Let's see if I've given the instructions clearly . . . "

Then, ask them if they have any questions to clarify the meaning. To further "lock in" the training, see that they use the training as soon as possible.

Skill of feedback

Use feedback in both positive and negative situations. Give positive feedback through recognition and compliments by letting others know when you like something they've said or done. These comments make people feel good about themselves.

Unfortunately, most of us ignore the good things people do or say, and concentrate on only the bad. Because this book is about dealing with difficult people, we'll be concentrating only on using it under negative or difficult situations. But don't forget the importance of positive feedback.

In feedback, you share your reactions to another person's behaviour, with that person. Use negative feedback if something someone has done has upset or irritated you. Discuss how you feel when others act or behave a certain way. People can't try to change their behaviour unless you let them know what their actions are doing to you.

You're not being fair to others if you don't communicate this to them. Letting negative situations build up, only escalates the difficulties between people. Resolve minor difficulties when they occur, don't just collect them for future blowups.

If we don't practice effective feedback, the following often results:

* Every time the person does anything that bothers us, a small blip occurs on our "screen of annoyance." If we don't deal with the problem or situation, and the person repeats their behaviour, this leads to,
* Another, bigger blip occurring on our "screen of annoyance." This does NOT have to be for the same reason as the original blip.
* Soon these blips collect, and we have a major blow-up with the person.

Even the most trivial incident can trigger this response. How much better it would be if we handled each blip immediately instead of recording it on our "screen of annoyance."

Feedback should be used to let others know when we:

* don't understand something they've said
* disagree with them
* think they've changed the subject or are going around in circles
* are getting irritated
* feel hurt or embarrassed

46

With feedback we can keep in touch with our feelings and can lessen problems associated with more serious negative feelings. This is when we feel, frustrated, angry, hurt, defensive, defeated, upset, afraid, depressed, dependent, weak, or defenceless, or any other negative feeling.

Guidelines for Giving feedback:

* Be selective when you use feedback. Ask yourself, *"Am I about to unload this beef properly? Is my reaction unfair or am I over-reacting?"*
* Remind yourself that the person must be able to do something about the situation.
* To be effective, there needs to be a foundation of trust between the sender and receiver of the feedback. Otherwise, the recipient could misinterpret the feedback as a personal attack. The recipient may hear only critical comments, and feel the need to defend him or herself rather than listen to what you have to say.
* Watch your timing, and don't dump too much criticism on a person at once.

Here are some guidelines for giving feedback:

(a) **Is The Receiver Ready?** Give the feedback only when there are clear signs the receiver is ready to listen to it. If they're not ready, the receiver won't hear your remarks or can misinterpret your comments.
(b) **Based on Facts - Not Emotions:** Giving feedback acts like a "candid camera." It's a report of the facts, rather than your ideas about why situations happened or what the person meant by them. *"You hurt Graham when you threw that toy."*
(c) **Happened Recently:** The closer you give feedback to the time the event took place, the better. If you give feedback immediately, the receiver is more likely to understand exactly what you mean. The feelings accompanying the event still exists so this, too, can help.
(d) **Timing Must Be Right:** Give feedback only when there's a good chance the person will listen to it. It may not be helpful

if the receiver feels there are other more pressing matters demanding his or her attention.

(e) **Protect Privacy:** Critical feedback given in front of others will be damaging rather than helpful.

(f) **Must be able to Change:** Feedback should be about situations that need changing, should the receiver choose to do so.

(g) **Freedom to Decide:** The receiver can consider whether s/he wishes to try a change after your feedback. You may wish to include that you'd like to see certain changes. You're not likely to be successful if you give the impression, *"I've told you what's wrong with you, now change!"*

(h) **Don't Give Too Much at Once:** When learning how to give feedback, we sometimes overdo it. It's as though we were telling the receiver, *"I just happen to have a list of beefs. Let me read them off to you."* The receiver would naturally prefer time to consider each item, and may balk at your overwhelming expectations.

(i) **Criticism Should be Helpful:** Always consider your motives for giving your opinions. Are you trying to be helpful to the receiver or are you unloading some of your feelings? Are you using the occasion to try to get the receiver to do something that benefits only you? For example, if you're angry and wish to express it - say so - but include a description of the behaviour that caused your anger.

(j) **Encourage them to Share Feedback:** Giving feedback can become "one-upsmanship." Because the giver has focused on the person's potential for improvement, the receiver goes away feeling as though s/he's "not as good." The receiver may feel as if you're giving him or her a lecture. The exchange will be better balanced if the giver includes some of his or her own feelings and concerns.

(k) **Be Specific - Not General:** Give quotes and examples of exactly what you're referring to.

Guidelines for receiving feedback:

(1) *State What you Want Feedback About:* This allows the giver of the feedback to feel you're open to hearing his or her reactions to your words.

(2) *Check what you've heard:* Use paraphrasing to be sure you understood the giver's message.

(3) *Share your reactions to the feedback:* As your feelings become involved, you may forget to share your reactions to the feedback you've received. Knowing what was and was not helpful, allows the giver to improve his or her skills at giving useful feedback. If s/he is uncertain about your reactions, s/he may be less apt to risk sharing in the future.

Process of Feedback

The three steps in the process of feedback are as follows:

PROCESS OF FEEDBACK

A. Describe the problem or situation to the person causing the difficulty.

B. Define what feelings or reactions (anger, sadness, anxiety, hurt, or upset) their behaviour causes you.

C. Suggest a solution or ask them to provide one.

Here's a sample situation:

Melanie's husband Jim had been late for dinner four nights in a week. He hadn't called, so she had held off serving dinner as long as possible. Her two pre-school children became cranky and restless and she finally fed them. She found that she became a clock watcher, getting more and more upset as the time passed and Jim hadn't arrived home.

In Melanie's case, she might have felt like saying, *"You're always late for dinner - can't you be on time for a change?"* This would only make Jim act defensively. Instead, she should try to gain his co-operation in solving the problem.

Melanie needs to let Jim know how she feels about his lateness. This would give him a chance to change his behaviour.

Using feedback, Melanie would say, *"Jim, when you don't call to let me know you're going to be late, it holds up dinner for the children. They get cranky and upset which in turn upsets me. It also means that I can't plan my evening. Because of this, I'd like you to call me if you're going to be late for dinner. Can I count on you to do this in the future?"*

A. The problem - Jim is late for dinner.

B. Her feelings or reactions - this upsets both her and their children.

C. Solution - she asks Jim to call if he's going to be late.

Here's another example:

Barry is an avid reader and enjoys curling up on the couch with a good book in the evenings. His wife Susan enjoys television, and shares the living room with him. She's very verbal and constantly interrupts his reading by making comments about the program she's watching. Barry becomes more and more annoyed as the evening progresses. He solves the problem of the interruptions by going into the kitchen (not as comfortable) or to their bedroom to read.

Susan complains that she never has time to talk to him except in the evening and feels abandoned when he "deserts" her and leaves the room. Both need to use feedback and make compromises.

Barry states, *"The reason I leave the room is because I can't concentrate on my book when you constantly interrupt me. This frustrates me more and more until I leave the room. Could you not interrupt me as much when I'm reading?"*

Susan, *"I feel deserted when you leave me alone. Can't we find a solution that is satisfactory to both of us?"*

Barry, *"It sounds as if you want us to have some private time together without the kids. Am I right?"*

50

"Yes, that really is the problem."
"Why don't we set aside time after dinner or before we go to bed when we can talk. Then you can enjoy your programs, and I can enjoy my book. How does that sound?"
"That sounds fine to me."

A. The Problems:
  - Susan is interrupting Barry's reading
  - Susan wants more communication from Barry

B. The feelings/reactions:
  - Barry gets annoyed when Susan interrupts his reading
  - Susan feels deserted by Barry

C. One Solution:
  - Private time so they can talk about important issues

Feedback steps

Most people will change undesired behaviour if it's brought to their attention in a kind, non-threatening way. But there are exceptions to the rule. Some just don't care what you think, they feel it's not worth changing to suit you, or they have a habit that's hard to change. Others change their behaviour for a while, but slip back to doing it their old way. In situations like that, further feedback steps are necessary.

In our example with Barry and Susan - life went along smoothly for two weeks, but Susan slipped back into interrupting Barry's reading while she watched her program. Using step two of feedback steps, Barry reminded Susan of their agreement.

When Susan did the same thing two nights later, Barry followed step three and asked, *"Susan can you tell me why you're still interrupting my reading, when you know it annoys me?"*

After she said, *"Oops, sorry,"* he replied, *"If it happens again I'll have no choice but to go to another room to read.*

51

Maybe we need to sit down again and discuss another approach to this problem. "

FEEDBACK STEPS

1. Follow (a), (b), and (c) steps from process of feedback.

2. Repeat #1.

3. (i) Ask person to explain why s/he's still doing something that s/he *knows* annoys you.

   (ii) Explain the consequences should the behaviour or situation happen again.

4. Follow-through with the consequences.

Feedback could be used to solve the following situations:
* When you come home tired from work, and find that Johnny's left a trail of his belongings from the back door to his room, or
* Family members leave their dirty clothes draped over the clothes hamper rather than in it, or
* Someone uses your tools and doesn't return them to the proper place.

Take a moment to identify the situations that bother you and how you could use feedback to eliminate them. Step 3 (where you make the person account for why they're doing something intentionally to annoy you) is very effective. With your children (if the fourth step is necessary) remember that the higher authority is YOU.

This is when you withdraw privileges, such as refusing to drive your son to his hockey game, or refusing to help your daughter to obtain a Brownie badge. Parents do many special things for their children. Just remove of these special things as "consequences," should their behaviour not change. **Make sure you follow through.**

Skill of listening

Another skill people take for granted, is listening. Attentive listening is a process that begins with the listener giving the speaker his or her undivided attention. This builds rapport and shows the speaker that the listener values what they're saying. If a speaker feels rushed (either by verbal or non-verbal hints) or if listeners appear too judgmental, they'll probably clam up.

Active Listening

You indicate you're interested and attentive to what someone is saying when:
1. Your body language shows you're listening - nodding your head, making eye contact, stopping what you're doing and concentrating on what they're saying.
2. Making "listening" noises such as *"I see . . . "*
   Or, *"Uh-huh . . . "*
   Or, *"That's interesting."*
3. Paraphrase what they've said to clarify understanding.
   Here are some facts concerning listening:
* We listen in spurts. Most of us are unable to give hard, close attention to what others say for more than sixty seconds at a time. We concentrate - we let up - then we concentrate again.
* We spend up to 80 per cent of our conscious hours using four basic communication skills; writing, reading, speaking and listening.
* Listening accounts for over 50 percent of that time, so we actually spend forty percent of our waking time just listening!
   Have you ever received specific training to show you how to listen? Probably not. As a student you probably heard, *"Patti will you stop talking . . . "* not *"Patti will you please listen."*
   How fast do you think the average person speaks in words per minute? (Keep in mind that secretaries usually take shorthand at 80-120 w.p.m. and court stenographers at 220 w.p.m.)
   Normal speaking speed is 125 - 150 w.p.m. My speaking speed is at least 160 w.p.m. especially when I'm conducting seminars.
   What do you think your thinking capability is in w.p.m.? I've heard guesstimates from 50 - 300 w.p.m. The average

person is capable of thinking at the phenomenal speed of 750 - 1,200 w.p.m.!

Then why don't we hear what people are telling us? Because our minds are bored - that's why. There's not enough happening to keep our brains occupied when people speak at normal speeds. Even my speed of 160 w.p.m., I can't always keep participants motivated. So what happens? My audience goes on side-trips (tune-outs) where they may:

--Find examples of something I'm discussing,
--Wonder why their spouse was in such a bad mood that morning,
--Admire an article of clothing and wonder where the person bought it,
--Think it must be time for a coffee break, because they're thirsty.

Unfortunately, they lose their train of thought and can get lost in their own thoughts.

Radio and television have turned most of us into a century of lazy listeners. For instance, did you turn the radio on this morning to catch the weather forecast? Did you hear it? Or did you tune out the voices, and miss it? It takes practice and concentration to keep "tuned in" to what others are saying. The next time you're listening to others, watch and see how often you "tune them out" during your communication with them.

How do you Rate as a Listener?

Rate yourself (or better yet, have a friend help you) using the following scale:

Always = 5   Almost always = 4   Sometimes = 3
Rarely = 2   Never = 1

1. Do I allow the other person to state his or her
   complete thoughts without interrupting?   ____
2. Do I listen to what others are saying "between
   the lines" using empathy to determine the real
   meaning of their words?   ____
3. Do I actively try to keep important facts?   ____

4. In a conference or important phone situation, do I
   I write down the most important details of a
   message?   ____
5. Do I avoid becoming upset or defensive if a
   speaker's views differ from mine?   ____
6. Do I repeat essential details of a conversation back
   to the speaker to confirm correct understanding?   ____
7. Do I exercise tact in keeping the speaker on track?
   (correct the problem without provoking retaliation?)   ____
8. Do I tune out distractions when I'm listening?   ____
9. Do I make an effort to show interest in the other
   person's conversation? (Make listening noises, nod
   my head).   ____
10. Do I understand that I'm learning little when I'm
    talking? (Do I talk too much, listen too little?)   ____
11. Do I sound as if I'm listening? (Use paraphrasing,
    ask questions?)   ____
12. Do I remember that people are less defensive when
    they feel you understand them?   ____
13. Do I understand that I don't always have to agree
    with the speaker?   ____
14. In personal conversation, do I look for non-verbal
    forms of communication?   ____
15. Do I look as if I'm listening in personal meetings?
    (Lean forward, give eye contact?)   ____
16. Do I ask for the spelling of names and places
    when I'm taking a message?   ____

Scoring: 64 or more - You're an excellent listener!
        50 - 63   - You're better than average
        40 - 49   - You require improvement!
    39 or less   - You're not an effective listener
                   practice, practice, practice!

Regarding question #16: whenever you're taking down
someone's name, ask them how to spell it (even the name
Smith, may be spelled Smythe). In brackets (below the spelling
of the name) add the phonetic pronunciation of the name. For
instance, the last name LEAHEY would be phonetically (Lay-hee);

KURLUIAK - (Curl-u-lack); PHOENIX - (Fee-nicks); URSALIAK - (Er-sal-uk).

Here's how you can improve your listening skills:

1. You must care enough to want to improve. Without this motivation, it'll be too much effort.
2. Try to find a quiet area in which to converse. Keeping your train of thought is difficult when there are obstructions to concentration.
3. Try to talk about matters that are of known interest to the other person.
4. Try not to anticipate what the other person will say.
5. Be mindful of your biases and prejudices, so they don't unduly influence your listening.
6. Pay careful attention to what they're saying without planning rebuttals to it.
7. Be aware of "red and green flag words" which trigger over-reaction. Examples of this are the phrases, "women's libber," or "male chauvinist."
8. Don't allow yourself to get too far ahead of the speaker by trying to understand information too soon.
9. At intervals, try to paraphrase what people have been saying. Give them the opportunity to learn what you think you've heard them say.
10. When you have difficulty determining the reasons for the conversation, ask *"Why are you telling me this?"*
11. Watch for key or buzz words if you find you've lost the train of the conversation. This usually happens when listening to long-winded people or those who ramble.
12. Analytical people have a difficult time in conversation. Their personal need to know every detail, might make the person who's in the conversation feel as if you're grilling them.

Qualities of a Good Listener

People who practice good listening skills practice the following techniques:

1. Let others finish what they're saying (they don't interrupt others).
2. If they don't follow the line of conversation, they ask questions.
3. They keep comfortable eye contact - don't let their eyes wander.
4. Pay attention to what others are saying.
5. Remain open-minded, ready to change their opinion.
6. Use feedback and paraphrasing skills.
7. Read others' non-verbal communication (body language) well.
8. Don't "tune out" inappropriately when others are speaking.

Stutterers

What errors do you think you commit when in conversation with someone who stutters? I'll bet you finish the sentence for that person. This forces the stutterer to explain that this was not what they were going to say, therefore making them start at the beginning again. Can you imagine the double annoyance this is for the stutter? Have a heart!

Here are a few matters to keep in mind when conversing with someone who stutters. Most stutterers are of either average or high intelligence. Their brains simply go too fast for their mouths to say what they want to say. Often, when they were children, parents and teachers encouraged them to speak faster, which only accelerated their problem. The more ridicule they received from others, the worse their problem became. A terrible "catch 22" situation.

Start by letting the stutterer know that you're willing to listen. Do this by practising good listening techniques. Give comfortable eye contact, nod your head, ask questions, and by all means let them finish what they're saying. Try to give the impression that you have time for them to say what they want to say. If you try to rush what they're saying, it just takes longer because of their nervousness.

Skill of speaking

Another communication skill we all need is the art of being able to say what we want to say. Verbal fluency enables us to express our thoughts clearly so others understand exactly what we mean. Because we're going to be talking the rest of our lives, if we have problems putting our thoughts into words, it certainly seems worth while to take steps to improve this skill. Otherwise we're allowing ourselves to remain handicapped in one of the most important communication skills of all.

How do you Rate as a Speaker?

Here is a test you can give yourself. As we often don't see ourselves clearly, it might be a benefit to have a friend do it for you as well. Rate yourself using the following scale:

Always = 5   Almost always = 4   Sometimes = 3
Rarely = 2   Never = 1

1. If I was a listener, would I listen to myself?   ___
2. If others have trouble understanding me, do I remember that it's my responsibility to help the other person understand me?   ___
3. Do I keep my instructions to others short, sweet and to the point?   ___
4. Can I determine when my audience has "Tuned me out?"   ___
5. Do I make sure my listeners know what I want from them?   ___
6. When I give instructions, do I ask for feedback and paraphrasing to make sure they understand me?   ___
7. Do I make sure my non-verbal communications are the same as my verbal ones?   ___
8. Do I make sure I don't intimidate my listeners?   ___
9. Do I speak clearly? (Do I mumble?)   ___
10. Do I use common language?   ___

Scoring: 40 or more - You're an excellent speaker!
          32 - 39   - You're better than average
          25 - 31   - You require improvement!
          24 or less - You're not an effective speaker.
                       Practice, practice, practice!

Did you chuckle to yourself when completing the first question? Did you find there was an element of truth in the question? If so, it's possible that you fit into one of three groups of people who believe that they're not worth listening to:

(a) They have trouble getting the words out. They know what they want to say, but can't quite say it (because they lack verbal fluency). They can improve this by joining Toastmasters or Toastmistress clubs or take a public speaking course.

(b) They're not up on what's going on. Often people insulate themselves from the terrible situations that are going on in the world. Suddenly, in social situations they may find they don't know what's going on, therefore they might feel they have nothing to contribute to the conversation. The solution is to catch up on what's happening.

(c) It's possible that they "run off at the mouth," have problems keeping conversations short, sweet, and to the point. They need to spend time organizing their thoughts before they speak. They can practice by writing down their thoughts, or use a tape recorder to catch themselves. Then they can practice rearranging their words using more precise language until they can say what they want to say without rambling.

If question three is a problem, (c) will help them as well. They would use the KISS principle:
* Keep it simple sweetie - or
* Keep it simple stupid (depending on how you feel at the time).

In question five, if they want something from someone or want their opinion, they should ask them for their help BEFORE they give them the background information. For example:

A man came home from work and wanted to discuss a work problem with his wife. She had just put in a rather tiring day herself. He proceeded to give her all kinds of details on what was happening, and surprised her out of half-listening by asking, *"What do you think I should do?"*

She was embarrassed, because she had not been paying attention. He had to repeat the entire commentary again. How much better it would have been, if he had started the conversation, *"Mary, I need your opinion on something that's*

59

happening at the office. Do you have time to discuss it right now?" Then he would have confirmed that she DID have time, and would have ensured her undivided attention.

CHAPTER 4
NON-VERBAL COMMUNICATION

Non-verbal communication

Being able to read others' non-verbal communication is probably one of the best assets anyone can have. We read others, more by what they're showing with their non-verbal communication or body language, than by anything they might say verbally.

What are you telling others by your non-verbal communication? Non-verbal communication, body language and the scientific study of kinesics all read a person's unconscious body movements and sounds. These signs include:

* Tone of voice
* Facial expression
* Posture
* Eye contact
* Touching
* Gestures
* Spacial distance
* Clothing

It's essential to *listen* to and understand others' non-verbal communication. The only people who can lie consistently with their body language (and get away with it) are con artists and compulsive liars. This is because even *they* believe the lies they're telling.

Our body language usually matches our personality. We can identify timid, uncertain people by the hesitant way they act. Their posture shows defeat, there's little eye contact, their voices are soft, their mannerisms nervous (nail biting, hand-wringing or hair twirling). They take up as little space as possible (pull all their "ends" in) or wear a fixed smile. Others cover their mouths when they speak or use nervous gestures such as touching their hair. Putting hands near the mouth, scratching their cheek or eyebrow says *"Don't listen to me. I'm not sure of what I'm saying"* or worse yet, *"I'm lying."* (even if they're not).

Colours make a difference too. When people aren't feeling well, they often announce this to others by wearing drab colours that can make them look even sicker.

We identify depressed people by their slumping posture, lack of eye contact and sad features. Self-confident people identify themselves by the way they carry themselves, make eye contact readily, their quick smile and ability to show emotion.

Examples of how we read body language:
* While having lunch with a friend, you notice that she has some food on the corner of her mouth. You'd like to bring this to her attention in a non-embarrassing way. You take your napkin and wipe YOUR face, but also, look at your friend's face where the food is. Automatically, she will wipe her face too, but couldn't explain why she did so.
* A person's posture shows how the person feels about him or herself or the situation.
* The person's body shrinks or slumps in on itself. (The person's tired, relaxed, or depressed).
* Person gives little eye contact. Often erroneously thought to show shifty behaviour, or lacking in self-confidence, which isn't always the case. This can indicate shyness, or can be cultural, where the person is showing respect to others who are elderly or are in positions of authority.
* European men cross their legs at the knee - Americans make a "4" with their legs.
* When we're interested in what others are saying, we'll lean forward, as we will when we wish to speak next.
* When zapped by a hard question, men are likely to clasp their hands in front of them in a "fig leaf" position; women cross their arms over their chests - both signals of feeling attacked.
* When people feel they're in a position of power, they often show dominance by deliberately interrupting others, stand with

feet straddled, hands on hips (parental stance). They use sarcasm to deflate others, or fail to step aside when on a collision course with others. They hold eye contact longer than is comfortable for the recipient, hover or lean over others while watching them.
* Men who want to show their power will put their feet up on a desk (but won't remove them when someone comes into the room). Power hungry people take up more space on chairs, couches or benches than is their due. Hair was traditionally associated with power, so the man who lovingly strokes his beard whenever the pretty waitress walks by is demonstrating power. He's not only showing power, but sexuality as well. As the waitress comes near his booth to refill his coffee, her stiffening posture and raised eyebrows show she's not impressed.

People-watching is cheap entertainment, because all you need is a little spare time - but what a learning experience it is! A good book on this topic is: *"Understanding Body Talk"* by Thomas G. Aylesworth.

The Handshake

We shake hands with people; an important non-verbal exchange. Originally, this communication meant that we were extending our empty weapon hand to them to show them that we came as a friend. Later it meant that we were giving them our word that the exchange to follow was above board and we were trustworthy.
Women should practice shaking hands with others until they feel comfortable extending a firm handshake.
Too often, when couples meet, the men shake hands, but the women don't. They should extend their hand and introduce themselves (if their partner hasn't already). *"Hello, I'm Mary Smith."*

Space Bubbles

We all have a "space bubble" of safety around us. For most people, this bubble extends about 18 - 24 inches away from their bodies. Filling your personal space by gesturing, will make you appear to be confident. On the other hand, folding your arms, slouching and making yourself small, signals timidity.

There are several normal distances we keep between ourselves and others. First there is:

Intimate Distance
Only people we trust are welcome within our "space bubble" (18 - 24"). This is more than physical distance, it's mental too. We welcome people who are near and dear to us into this space, but we often have to endure others as well. This can be at the theatre, on a bus, at a seminar, or in an elevator. There are hundreds of instances where we have to tolerate this closeness.

Watch others when you're in an elevator. Do they pull in all their *"ends"* and take up as little space as possible? Heaven forbid, should they touch the person next to them, they'll automatically state, "Oops, sorry," and pull away. This also would happen if they touched someone in a theatre lineup, or at a checkout counter. In elevators, as soon as the crowd thins, people will automatically make more room between them.

Personal Distance.
This is the space people usually keep with others when they have enough room to be comfortable. This is anywhere between two and a half and four feet depending on their comfort zone and how well they know the person. Then there's:

Social Distance.
This is four to seven feet away from others. This could be sitting on chairs or couches facing each other.

Far Social Distance.
This could happen at a large party or be the distance between a speaker and his or her audience.

Territorial Supremacy

Not only do we have "space bubbles" around us, but ownership extends to anything we think belongs to us. This may be our bedroom, kitchen or workshop, our car or boat, or our brush and comb. Others may use these articles only when we've given them permission to do so. This is why we react so violently when someone takes something that belongs to us without permission.

People have a psychological upper hand when they're in their own "territory." This is why people are most comfortable in their own surroundings - on their own "turf." The next most comfortable space is somewhere neutral (such as a restaurant, a beach or a place that doesn't "belong" to either person). The least comfortable place (as far as comfort is concerned) is normally the other person's "turf." Keep this in mind should you expect a confrontation with another person. If possible, have the confrontation on your "turf."

Eye Contact

Eye contact is more than just eye contact. It's more like face contact. You watch the person's expressions, read lips, etc. to pick up what they're saying. Comfortable eye contact is three seconds, then the person looks away. If you hold eye contact longer than three seconds, you'll invade another's body space, as easily as if you had touched them. Many aggressive people use this to intimidate others. They could be fifty feet away from you, but you'll still feel this person's invasion of your space.

You may remember using it yourself when you've been very angry with someone. You looked them right in the eye as you spoke to them. If a person says, *"He was shooting darts at me,"* that person was probably giving full eye contact for longer than three seconds. He probably had a mean expression on his face to reinforce the extended eye contact.

Be aware that a person's gender can affect the amount of eye contact they exchange. When a woman is talking to a man, she'll look him in the eye when HE is speaking to her, but not when SHE is speaking to him. Blinking eyes could mean the person is lying or they could be nervous. Non-blinking eyes with eye contact could mean the person is lying, and watching for the other person's reaction. Don't jump to conclusions, because they might only be very interested in what you have to say.

A wink could show intimacy or lack of seriousness. You'd use this when you're telling a "white lie" to a child, and want his or her parents to know you're doing so.

When you want to sway a group to your point of view, or when you're selling something, unflinching eye contact is essential. When being criticized, try to maintain eye contact without squinting - a normal defensive action that portrays the expression *"Oh yeah, we'll see about that!"*

Smiling

Not all smiles are the same. There are subtle physical differences in authentic smiles and those "put-on" for someone else's benefit. The true smile of enjoyment involves movement around the lips, the muscle around the eye contracts (pulling the skin down between the eyebrow and the eyeball) and the eyebrow lowers slightly.

The insincere or counterfeit smile does not include the movement of the skin around the eyes. As well, the lips may narrow, or the upper lip may curl.

There's nothing wrong with smiling if it compliments your spoken message, but if your smile is nervous or forced, you'll give garbled signals. In primates, smiling and grinning are gestures of appeasement used by weaker animals as a way of asking for gentler treatment from more powerful animals. In humans, it's often the way used to soften a message. But when people smile while speaking seriously, the message is, *"Please like me."* This eagerness to please can come across as uncertainty.

Lying

When people are proud of what they've accomplished, they're open with their body language. They show their hands openly. When they feel guilty or suspicious, they hide their hands either in their pockets or behind their back. If you accuse them of something, they'll likely give you an incredulous look and reply, *"Who me?"* To try to make you believe them more they'll usually put their hand on their chest (a non-verbal sign of honesty). The hand to the chest gesture when used by women is a protective gesture showing sudden surprise or shock.

Additional body language identifies whether the person is lying. Watch for a combination of these:

- They'll not look at you (look down usually)
- Blink their eyes rapidly
- Twitch and swallow repeatedly
- Clear throat and wet lips often
- Cover mouth when speaking
- Shrug shoulders
- Rub nose
- Scratch head while talking
- Put hand on throat
- Rub back of their neck

The last sign is the most obvious sign of lying in men. It can also mean that he's exasperated with the situation, so don't jump to conclusions.

Habits

We're all creatures of habit. You might get a chuckle over trying the following, (this won't work for those who live alone). Sit at someone else's place at the table or where others normally sit while watching TV. Don't say anything - just do it and watch their discomfort.

When you're visiting elderly people, you'll know when you're sitting in someone's favourite chair by observing their body language. Please offer them their favourite chair.

Start poking about in a woman's kitchen, and you'll hear comments such as, *"Where did you put the colander away."* In a man's workshop you'll hear, *"Who's been into my toolbox."* If anything's out of place, they'll notice it.

To Touch or Not to Touch

We often place our hand on the arm or shoulder of an upset person. If they're a close friend, relative, child, or elderly person, we might put an arm around their shoulder or hug them to give comfort.

The book *"The Silent Language,"* by Dr. Edward T. Hall, shows that conditioning and cultural backgrounds strongly affect our body language responses. If you deal with people of other cultures, it's a book well worth reading.

For instance, Italian people touch much more often than those in North America who back away from this perceived familiarity. They think of Italian people as pushy and in turn, Italians think of them as cold or reserved.

People from Arabia think of a person as a point somewhere deep inside the body - therefore they often stand extremely close and yet do not feel they're invading anyone's privacy. In fact, they consider it polite to stand close enough to breathe on each other while talking. They also must converse face to face, and find it difficult carrying on a conversation while walking side by side with a companion.

When people are hospitalized, two of the things they dislike the most are the feelings of isolation and lack of comforting physical touching. They're in unfamiliar territory (not their "turf") may feel apprehensive, frightened, and afraid of what will happen or has already happened to them.

This is when a caring pat on the shoulder, or a friend holding a hand is not only welcomed, but often necessary for a speedy recovery. Nothing combats the loneliness of being in the hospital, like having loved ones provide their comforting touch when needed. Fill that need, whenever you visit anyone in the hospital. Even a casual friend welcomes a pat on the arm or some other physical gesture that shows you care.

Arguments

Should you have to referee an argument, put your body language knowledge to the test. If you notice there are observers to an argument, they may not want to get involved or express an opinion. They will anyway, because their body language will tell you what they believe, and whose side they're on. If they've had the opportunity of learning all the facts about the case, they'll automatically take sides. When this happens, they'll copy the body language of the person they think is in the right.

The more observers there are, the better it will be, because they'll unknowingly choose sides. You'll then have a running start if you're responsible for refereeing the argument.

Use of intuition, gut reaction and hunches

Occasionally, when we read another person's body language, another non-verbal communication skill kicks in. Women call this skill intuition. Most men call it their "gut reaction" or they have a "hunch." Suddenly, they have the feeling that they really should - or should not - do something, although they can't identify why they feel that way. They try to find facts to explain their feeling, but they often can't.

Many of us scoff at this flash of information, and discount our intuitive feelings because we can't find any facts to back up our reactions. I had this phenomenon explained this way. We have two brains (no, I'm not referring to the left/right brain theory). One is our conscious brain. It keeps up-to-date data available for easy reference. I think of this as my brain's computer software.

The other is our subconscious brain which is far superior to the conscious brain. It holds all our memories - those we consciously remember, and those we've buried in the back recesses of our minds. I think of this as my hard disk. I'd be crazy if I didn't use the best equipment available to me (my subconscious brain), because it has a memory bank far superior to my lower-grade software (conscious brain). When I listen to my intuition, I'm using my hard disk which has a superior memory bank. Doesn't it make sense to listen to the better one?

Sometimes when we have intuitive feelings, we may wonder how we came up with the strong convictions that often accompany our intuitive thoughts.

For instance, you find yourself suddenly feeling uncomfortable around another person. You may even feel threatened, and yet when you consciously examine the person, you can't determine why you feel your unease.

Should you be listening to your intuitive feelings? Of course you should! When it tells you something - listen to it because it's seldom wrong. The only time I haven't listened to my intuition was when I took an instant dislike to someone. After standing back, I realized that this person physically resembled another person I disliked and distrusted. By turning off my intuitive feelings, I learned that the person was okay.

You can probably recall when something about a person upset you and our instincts said to watch out. You may or may not have listened to these instincts, and possibly suffered the consequences.

CHAPTER 5
MARRIAGE PROBLEMS

Pre-marital counselling

It takes most of us many years of training to prepare for our careers, but how much training do we obtain to prepare us for two of the most important events in our lives - choosing a mate and having a family?

When a couple marry, they leave behind thinking only for and of themselves and change most aspects of their existing lives. Now they faced life together, united by love but remaining two distinct individuals. As a couple, they'll confide in each other, depend upon each other, have new responsibilities to each other, create new family ties, develop a stable home, and bring forth the signs of their love - their children.

The main ingredient for a successful marriage, is giving unquestioning trust and love to each other. This means not only sharing ideas, but being open and honest with each other. Couples accomplish this by being in touch with what's really going on inside themselves and being willing to share those feelings with each other. This eliminates manipulation, and results in honest, DIRECT communication.

There are many questions a couple should ask themselves before they take the big step into marriage. Unfortunately, if couples don't have a strong religious affiliation, they often run into a dead-end, trying to find someone who will offer pre-marital counselling. Couples are often in for a big surprise, if they neglect to ask crucial questions about what they expect out of their relationship. Here are the questions couples should discuss BEFORE getting married. Each partner should answer them separately, then discuss each question together, and compromise where necessary.

* Do you feel we should live together before we get married?
* How long should we know each other before considering marriage?
* What kind of wedding will we have - large, small, house of worship, Justice of the Peace?
  - Where will we hold our wedding (what city, town, church)?
  - How many will we invite?
  - Will we both invite an equal number of guests?
  - Who will stand up for us?
  - Who will be paying for which marriage expenses?
  - Where and how will we spend our honeymoon?
* What is your view of marriage commitment?
* What do you hope marriage will offer you that you don't have now?
* Where will we live: in an apartment, home, with friends, family?
  - Which city or town?
* What kind of job will you have?
  - Will you travel with your job?
  - Might we have to move because of future job prospects?
* How do you feel about wives/mothers having paid employment?
  - Do you think the wife should stay home with the children?
  - When would you approve of the wife returning to work?
  - How would you feel if the wife made more money than the husband?
  - How would you feel if the wife's company wanted her to move to another city?
* Will you share your outside interests and work with me?
* How would you feel if your spouse had to return to school for several years and you were the sole breadwinner?
* How much money will we have to live on? Your salary? Mine?
* How do you spend your money?
* How much of our budget should we spend on fun?
* How often would you like to entertain: your friends, my friends?

* How do you use credit?
- What amount of money do you owe now?
- How will we use credit in the future?
* How do you feel we should handle our paycheques and bills?
* Do you want to manage the money, or should I?
- Will we keep a budget? If so, do you know how to keep one?
* Should we have joint or separate bank accounts?
* How much money will you have to spend on yourself each week?
* How much money will I have to spend on myself each week?
- Who will decide this?
* How do you like spending your leisure time?
* Should we both have an equal voice in all family decisions?
* What are your views on birth control?
- What method would you want to use?
- What are your views on abortion?
* How many children do you want?
- Do you want boys or girls?
- When would you like to start a family? If a child was to come before that time, how would you feel?
- What if we couldn't have our own, would you want to adopt?
- Would you treat that child as if it was yours?
- How much time are you willing to give to the actual upbringing of our children?
- Would you be willing to get up at night to care for our children?
- What duties would you not be willing to do in the care of our children?
- If our child was born with a deformity, a disability or mentally retarded, would you accept the child? Would you love the child less than a normal child?
* Describe what you think your parenting style would be?
- Who should discipline our children?
* How often do you like to eat out?
* Do you like to cook?
* How much housework would each of us do?
* Do you have any disabilities that I don't know about?
* Do you have to take medication for any chronic illness?
* How is your general physical health?
* Have you ever had a criminal record?
* Do you like to gamble?

* Are you a safe driver? Ever drink and drive or drive unsafely?
* Should we keep liquor in our home? Why?
* Are you going to continue smoking (if applicable)?
* Do you snore? (This has caused many a marriage break-up)
* Are you an overly neat or messy person?
* Are you a morning or night person?
* Would you describe yourself as frugal or do you spend freely?
* How often would we go on holidays? How and where would we spend them?
* Do you have a car? How much is owing on it?
* Do you have a will? Are you willing to prepare one as soon as we get married?
* Do you have any life insurance? Should we get some? How much?
* What religion will we follow (if any)? How much time, energy and effort will this involve.
* What possessions will you bring into our home?
  - What items do you feel we have to buy for our home? How much money will we need for this?
* How important to you is the expression of affection?
  - Are you a romantic (flowers, love notes, etc.) type of person?
  - Do you like to be touched - in public - only where there's privacy?
  - Do you believe in pre-marital intercourse?
  - How often would you like to have intercourse?
  - How long does it take you to become aroused and how is this accomplished?
  - How long should love-making last?
  - How experimental do you like to be?
* Describe your moods - are you often depressed or frustrated?
  - How do you deal with negative feelings?
  - When you feel troubled, do you share your problems or withdraw?
  - How much "private time" do you normally need?
  - Describe your basic personality (outgoing/introvert).
  - Do you like being with friends or prefer being alone or with family members?
* Do you like to have music or the radio on, or do you like it best when it's quiet?
* How do you settle arguments?
  - How vocal are you during arguments?

- How often are you willing to give in?
- If you have feelings of rage and anger, how do you deal with them?
- How often do you say things that you wish you could take back?
- Are you a good loser or do you hold a grudge?
- Do you fight fair?
- Do you ever solve difficulties with violence?
* How do you deal with stress?
* Would you describe yourself as a jealous person? If so, how do you deal with jealousy?
* What would you do if I had an affair with someone else?
* Do you believe in remaining faithful, even when situations aren't going well?
* Do you feel comfortable giving and receiving compliments?
* Do you need continual reassurance from the important people in your life?
* How do you rate your listening skills?
* How do you act then others don't listen to you?
* Do you interrupt others? Do they get annoyed?
* Do you say one thing, but mean another?
* Do you feel comfortable discussing your innermost feelings with me?
* Do you ever use the "silent treatment" to get your way?
* Do you use hurting sarcasm when you feel defensive?
* Can you say what you want to say, when you want to say it (verbal fluency)?
* How do you get along with your parents: brothers and sisters, other relatives?
- How often do you see them?
- How often would we visit them - they visit us?
- What kind of childhood did you have?
- Did you come from a dysfunctional home? Explain.
* When we're married, how much time will you spend with "the girls/boys?"
* How do you view my friendship with others of the opposite sex?
- Would you object to my seeing them alone?
* What is it that attracts you to me?
* What qualities of mine would you hope I would change?
- What qualities of yours do you think you should change?

* If I suddenly became paralyzed or disfigured, how would you feel?
* If I died first, would you remarry?
* If you died first, would you expect me to remarry?

Second Marriages:

* If step-children are involved - how does the step-parent get along with your children?
 - If there's hostility, will counselling be necessary?
 - How does the natural parent feel about the step-parent disciplining his or her children?
 - What part does the divorced parent play in the step-child's life? Could there be potential problems?
 - How can you resolve these problems?
 - What other problems will the step-parent likely have to face with existing step-children?
 - Will we live in your home, my home, or find another?
 - Are you impotent, frigid?

For my married readers: How many of the above questions did you discuss with your spouse before marriage? Were there any you know you should have discussed, because there have been problems?

How prepared are you for the second part - having a family? Do you have enough experience on how to bring up a child? Did you have younger brothers and sisters to practice on? Did you babysit other parent's children to learn about childcare? Both potential parents should have had exposure to childrearing. If they don't, they should get this exposure by being around other parents with children to observe how they handle their children. Many community centres offer child-care classes that prepare parents for their offspring.

When a couple's first child arrives, many husbands believe their wives pay more attention to their babies than to them. Often the couple's sex life doesn't get back to normal until a full year after the birth of their child. If the wife is struggling along on four hours sleep a night, the natural outcome is that she's likely too tired for sex at any time.

This is why it's so important for the husband to help his wife with the myriad of new duties that go with the baby's arrival. This includes getting up with the child during the night or making sure that someone else does. Then, if both work together, they'll have more time for each other.

Keeping the home-fires burning

A man and a woman are, and always will remain, individuals. Marriage doesn't change this fact. It can only be strong if each partner is strong as an individual.

Many problems erupt that involve the upkeep of the home. Many men have such a stressful time at work that they have little or no energy left to help at home. Many young fathers put in long hours either at work, or bring home mountains of more work. There's nothing left at the end of the day for household and childcare responsibilities. It's possible that one or both of them, don't have time to do their share of the home, yard, and child care tasks. The person in this position should hire someone to do their portion of the work or pay other members of the family to do it. The person requiring the help pays the salary of the helper despite whether it's the husband or the wife.

Other, less busy husbands exclaim, *"What do you mean - I help you around the house!"* This is the same husband that, when his wife goes back to work, "helps" around the house by taking the garbage out once a week. In reality, he's not "helping his wife" - he's helping himself - simply doing part of his share.

Breadwinner/child and home care roles

Traditionally a man's job was to be THE BREADWINNER. The woman's job was HOME AND CHILD CARE. Now that women are sharing the breadwinner duties, they believe that men should share the home and child care as well. Surveys indicate that today, men are doing slightly LESS housework than they did in the 1970's. The men tried it, and didn't like it. Working women still spend an average of 2.5 hours a day to a man's one hour a day doing chores around the home.

Many working wives wonder how they can keep up with their double workload. An unshakable fact, is that many men's lives are made a lot easier because they come home to a caring, nurturing, empathetic partner. This partner is called a "wife." It's unfortunate that every working woman doesn't have this luxury as well. If they did, they'd lose half their frustrations and feelings that there's "something missing." in their lives.

Men are learning that nurturing doesn't have to be an exclusively feminine trait, but can be a very masculine characteristic as well. These are the husbands who see their wives come dragging home from work, and say, *"Had a tough day? How about a cup of tea?"* Or, *"Do you want half an hour to yourself while I fix dinner?"* Isn't this what good wives traditionally do for their husbands?

Women's Movement

Women such as Betty Friedan and Germaine Greer were the vanguard of the modern women's movement. They shocked the world by resisting inequality and challenging those in authority to accept women's equality. Their shock tactics worked, and women in the eighties and nineties are very thankful for their pioneering courage.

Research tells us that when men with traditional views marry, most have no intention of changing the routine of their lives. They figure that, they'll do the same things, think the same things, and be the same person, but as a married rather than a single man. In the past, women have often reshaped their personalities to conform to the wishes, needs and demands of their husbands. This is drastically changing in most households.

Traditionalist husbands believe there should only be one breadwinner in the family and he'll lose face if his wife goes to work. In these homes, even if they do work outside the home, the women continue to do most household chores and child rearing.

The belief that the family unit is breaking down is becoming increasingly widespread, and the return of women to the work force is often cited as the cause of this breakdown. The premise was that women were so harried from handling their dual roles that they were all stressed out. In families where everyone works as a team, this is just not so. In the past, when women stayed at home with their children, the children seldom, if ever, helped out around the home; that simply wasn't their job.

When mothers work away from the home, everyone pitches in, which builds responsibility and teamwork in the children.

Research states that perhaps women got the message early on in their lives, that they could handle the home and employment fronts as long as they spent enough effort. This was happening while the men are taking on the mundane home chores they had no training for, that they disliked, and never expected to perform in their lives.

Although many favourable changes have occurred, it's a constant battle to overcome and change the still-existing inequities. For instance, just recently, courts offered judges special courses to eliminate bias against females in their courtrooms. Many companies in Canada are ignoring a Supreme Court of Canada decision requiring them to pay sick leave benefits for part of a woman's pregnancy leave. Insurance companies aren't providing benefits in line with this decision.

The Court ruled in 1989, that companies have an obligation to extend sick leave benefits to pregnant female employees if their health requires them to stay away from work. Employers rely on the ignorance of employees who are often not aware of their rights. Until they receive complaints, there's no incentive for insurance companies to pay up.

Damned if they do - Damned if they don't

Some women feel guilty because they stay at home after they have children. Some who return to work, feel guilty because they did. Many women admit that they wouldn't go back to work full time if they could afford not to do so.

Their husbands may still encounter comments such as, *"How come your wife went back to work - don't you earn enough with your salary?"*

When some women return to work they hear statements such as, *"You can't go back to work, your kids need you, depend on you . . .,"* Or, *"Why did you have kids in the first place if all you wanted was to educate yourself and go back to work?"* Their parents, in laws, and non-working female friends in the neighbourhood may offer a variety of guilt-generating reasons why women shouldn't return to work or go back to school for upgrading. Women need to recognize that others don't have the right to tell them what they should or shouldn't do with their lives. The mothers themselves, are the only ones equipped to decide.

Psychological studies show that children of working mothers develop as well as (and sometimes better) than children with full-time mothers. It's how much a woman loves her children, how concerned and involved she is with them, and how happy she is with her life (not whether she works or stays home) that's important.

Men's Movement

But what about the men? How have they adapted to the changes caused by the women's movement? Many men agree that it's about time there's more protection for women and children against abuse and inequities. However, for many others, there's a men's movement underway. These are men who like the idea of being men, but aren't sure they're going about it the right way. The definition of what it means to be a man has changed almost as fast as the idea of what it means to be a woman.

Most men learned how to be a man from their mothers. As one man explained to me, *"Men, to some degree, are afraid of women and hold them in awe. When you think about it, this is not too unique an idea. Most of us have had mothers, who in the early part of our lives were responsible for all our needs and could give (or withhold) affection and approval. And since mothers are the earliest model for how we deal with women, it follows that we feel a bit inferior to them. This may be the root cause of most of the put-downs that women experience and for the abuse of women that is so pervasive in our society."*

Not only are men confused about the changes they see happening to women, but they also feel a sense or rage at how their fathers handled life. They remember that though their fathers might have been going through a crisis, his children never heard of it - because their father kept insisting that everything was "all right." Even though they may have been laying awake at night wondering how they could make ends meet, why they didn't get the promotion, or why their company transferred them again, everything was still "all right." These fathers clammed up when it came to letting their wives and children know what was

80

really happening out there. These fathers had accepted what they saw as their burden as men - to make life appear easier for their family than it really was. What a lonely existence those fathers had!

Most men's fathers came home tired from work, became shadowy figures behind their newspaper, sports and news broadcasts. The result of this, is that men didn't learn how to have close trusting relationships with other men (or women for that matter).

Thousands of men are finding their fathers' withdrawal and silence maddening enough to join groups of other men to discuss the myriad of problems facing them. Their discussions revolve around parental abuse, fatherly neglect, the women's movement, and emotional uncertainty about what's happening in the world. Many of these "gatherings" involve not only blue-collar workers, but lawyers, salesmen, and accountants.

A book (called the New Man's bible) entitled *"Iron John"* (a best-seller) identifies men's "inner warriors" and identifies men's sense of outrage at the changes in society. Poet Robert Bly's best selling book of poems, imply that males are out of touch with their basic manly feelings. It concentrates on the passing of the good days when fathers taught their sons the masculine arts of sowing, reaping, and pillaging.

Another best selling book is Sam Keen's *"Fire in the Belly: On Being a Man,"* which suggests that to find themselves, men must separate themselves from women. The anti-movement movement attempts to get men back, what they feel they lost by the women's movement.

The transition hasn't been easy for women and neither has it been for men. We have to wonder at the advantages perceived by turning the clock back to the paternalistic society of the early 1900's.

Spousal problems

Mundane, everyday occurrences and troubles can add up between couples. Unless they deal with the little problems, they accumulate and end up being big ones. Here are examples of problems many couples face:

Two-career couple

"We need help. My wife and I have a six-month-old son. She recently returned to work and we're having a terrible time adjusting to the changes we both have to make. It's a constant struggle to get everything done, and we both have to keep a running log on who does what throughout the day to get everything done. We're both frazzled and wonder if it's all worth it."

Both of you need to separate work and home. Practice a routine. Start by cleaning up your work area before you leave, signifying to yourself that you're leaving one set of responsibilities for another. Try to avoid traffic jams. Escape from pressures during your travel home. Listen to music, buy books on tape and play them while you're driving or riding home or meditate for several minutes on the bus or train.

If you have children at home, be as prepared as you can for their onslaught. Give them a nourishing snack while you change out of your work clothes. Have one of their favourite videotapes ready to pop into the VCR so they won't immediately besiege you with their gripes and concerns. Occasionally, take time out for yourself. Have a night out with the boys or girls while your partner tends to the needs of the children.

Most employers haven't moved with the times. With over half the families as dual earners, there's nobody at home to look after the home front. If one of the dual-earners has to work overtime, it can throw a wrench into the works. Whatever the parent decides to do (work overtime, or go home to care for the kids) they end up feeling guilty about what they're not doing.

Dual wage earners need to be flexible, and have good communication with the other partner (or have a substitute partner if you can't reach the original). Call a neighbour to ensure the child is cared for until a parent gets home, etc.

Here's an example of a situation that happened to a childless couple:

Joe and Della have been married just over a year. Normally, he arrives home from work before his wife. They have an agreement that the first one home starts dinner, but today everything "hit the fan" at work and he's very tired. As he enters his home, memories of having his mother meet him at the door and stroking his brow and bringing him nourishment invades his mind.

He shakes himself out of his nostalgia, reminding himself that he has decisions to make. Both he and Della forgot to take something out of the freezer for dinner that morning. He contemplates whether he should call to have Chinese food delivered.

What he really feels like doing, is jumping into his jacuzzi and soaking for fifteen minutes. The more he thinks about it, the more appealing this alternative becomes. He promises himself, *"I'll just indulge myself for fifteen minutes, then I'll tackle the dinner problem."*

He fills the tub, pours himself a drink, and his ears are underwater, filled with the sound of the gushing faucet, when he feels through the water the reverberation of a door slamming. He turns off the water, hears nothing, and settles down again in the soothing water. Five minutes later, a voice in the doorway announces Della's arrival.

"I've really had a tough day. My boss still is unhappy with my latest project." she says with a sigh. *"I really need a shower, some TLC (tender, loving care) and a massage. Move over, I'm coming in. What - you're getting out? Did you order anything for dinner? No Chinese for me, okay. I'm starving for pizza."*

Welcome to the splendid world of the two-career couple, where both have something to say, but no one wants to listen. Couples have to learn where their priorities lie, and remind themselves of their first loyalty - to each other and their separate needs. They need to set contingency plans where both work hard to stay in tune with the needs of the other, and deal with situations like this.

Destructive in-fighting

Sometimes we hurt the people we're closest to - spouses, children, and close friends because we use "in-fighting" tactics to solve disagreements. This is when you have privileged information that enables you to get behind the person's veneer - how to get them where it hurts - where they're vulnerable. And they retaliate by doing the same to you. When you feel tempted to give someone a low blow, or "rub their noses in old

83

wounds," contemplate the fall-out. Once the words are out, you can't retract them, and they might come back to haunt you in the future.

Another serious problem is that couples refuse to listen to the other person's side of an argument. Think about the last rip-snorting argument you had with someone close to you. Were you really listening to what the other person said? Or were you busy formulating your ideas so you could defend your side of the issue?

Good communication can save a relationship from being pulled apart by hurt, angry feelings. Listening with love means that you care and give attention to what your partner is saying (instead of what you expect to hear). Because we communicate not only with words, but through signs and gestures (body language) watch what your body is telling others.

Disagreements can even strengthen relationships provided the combatants learn to listen carefully to each other. The following techniques are very effective, as long as couples discuss these steps BEFORE they have an argument, not during it.

When tempers flare one or the other gives a signal (this could be a raised hand giving a "stop" or "time-out" signal). Then, they follow these steps:

Dissolving disagreements

1. They flip a coin to decide who will speak first.
2. Person #1 speaks; Person #2 does nothing but listen and occasionally ask questions that will clarify what Person #1 says.
3. When Person #1 says all s/he wishes to on the topic, Person #2 paraphrases what s/he believes the other person has said. Person #1 either agrees, or clarifies with more explanation.
     Under no circumstances should Person #2 defend his or her side of the situation.
4. Person #1 identifies how s/he feels when the situation happens.
5. Person #2 acknowledges and paraphrases what Person #1 says about how s/he feels.
6. Person #1 explains what s/he thinks will solve the situation.

7. Person #2 paraphrases what s/he hears Person #1 say about solutions to the problem.
8. They repeat the process with Person #2 having the opportunity of expressing his or her views.
9. The couple agrees on how they will deal with the problem in the future.

They continue this process until they have discussed all the problem situations. As you can see, there must be considerable give-and-take in this exchange, but listening and empathizing with each other are essentials for the process to work.

Swapping Complaints

From time to time, husbands and wives should have "gripe" sessions where they discuss annoying things their spouses do. Both must be willing to accept the other's criticism. Then they should explain what they'd like their partners to do in place of their annoying actions. For example:

A husband leaves his dirty clothes in a pile in the bedroom or on top of the clothes hamper - the wife explains where she wants him to put his dirty clothes.

A wife is a terrible procrastinator (the husband is very organized and punctual) - the husband explains how he feels when she's late and suggests solutions to her lateness.

"Sniping"

"When I visit a couple I know, I find myself very uncomfortable when they 'snipe' at each other. This happens when they make remarks that they gear towards chipping little pieces off the self-esteem of the other. What should I do when they start doing this in my presence?"
The more a marriage is in trouble, the more sniping there seems to be. Sniping includes the following:

1. One partner is telling a story. The other spouse keeps interjecting with corrections to the story.
2. The person makes disparaging comments related to the other sex, forcing the partner to defend his or her gender.
3. Starts fights in public or in front of friends or family.

4. Play one-upsmanship and competes openly with his or her partner.
5. Something went wrong, so it has to be because of something the other partner did (scapegoat and/or pass-the-buck).
6. Won't admit s/he's wrong when s/he is.
7. If the other partner wins at a game, s/he becomes cranky or sulks.
8. If their partner wants some privacy or space, s/he follows the other around asking *"What's wrong?"* and won't leave them alone to think things out.
9. Sets up their partner by making comments such as, *"Wait until your Mother/Father gets home!"*
10. Holds grudges, pouts and gives others the silent treatment.
11. Makes cutting, sarcastic remarks.
12. Makes fun of how his or her partner looks, what s/he wears, things s/he does.

When couples do this in your presence, explain how you feel when they snipe at each other. *"When you act like that towards each other, I feel very uncomfortable. Can you tell me why you feel the need to be so cruel to each other?"* If they continue to use this behaviour, explain that you're going to leave rather than watch their cruelty to each other. Then, do it!

Their behaviour could be the result of boredom, the need to put their spouse down, a power struggle, or all of these. It's a kind of disease that seldom improves, unless the couple acts to stop it. Whatever the causes are, it's a form of torture that gives bad "vibes" to the other person and constantly picks away at their self-esteem. Someone has to stop it, or it will continue and probably escalate into divorce or violence. Counselling is often the only solution.

Divorce

"My wife and I are divorcing. How should we tell our children?"
This is a difficult task. Whenever possible, both parents should break the news to their children. The sooner the better, rather than take the chance that they'll hear it from someone else. Keep your comments short to lessen the anxiety.

You might start by saying, *"Mommy and Daddy have decided that they don't get along any more. It has nothing to do*

86

with you, and we'll both continue to love you. We just can't live together any more, so I'll be moving to an apartment not too far from here."

The older the child or teen, the more intense might be their reaction. They may be more vocal and angry and will have questions they need answered. Be candid and honest with your answers. Many might lash out at the parents to express their hurt at what's happening. Younger children may simply cry and cling to the parent who's leaving. They feel out-of-control of the situation and have the anxieties to match.

Make sure they know they're not the cause of the divorce. It's important for parents to realize the way children think. Children somehow believe that they're responsible for all the good and bad situations that happen around them. Parents might have to initiate this subject, because sometimes the children haven't even formulated the idea in their minds enough to talk about it. It may just be a feeling they have, that they were responsible.

Other children might not react at all until they've had an opportunity to digest the changes. Give them an opportunity to ask questions that concern them. Be empathetic, realizing how terrible they might be feeling and try to allay the fears they may have about how their life might change. Both parents should be available and honest with their children.

Questions children will inevitably ask will be:
1. Will we have to move to another home?
2. Will I still have a room of my own?
3. Will we still have skating, piano and hockey lessons?
4. Can we still go camping next year?
5. Will we have to go to a new school?

It's surprising the number of irrelevant questions the child might appear to ask. None are frivolous, so deserve honest answers. Be willing to let your children know that you're hurting too. It's all right to cry and explain that you're sad.

When asked why you don't love each other any more, what are you going to answer? Keep your antagonism to each other out of your answer. You might say, *"We fight too much."* Or, *"We aren't happy living together any more."* Watch that you don't reinforce the idea that you don't love each other any more, otherwise they might feel that you could stop loving them as well (causing more anxiety).

CHAPTER 6
DIFFICULT HUSBANDS

This chapter concentrates on problems wives have with their husbands.

Possessive father

"My husband is very possessive of our teenaged children. He stifles them, has to know exactly where they are and everything about their lives. He restricts them from participating in normal teenage activities. Our children are becoming rebellious and our home is becoming a battleground."

Domineering parents are often one-dimensional people who make parenting their sole reason for being alive. They hang onto their children because they'd lose all sense of identity and meaning if they let them go their own ways. What's really happening is that the parent is trying to get his or her needs met at the child's expense.

These parents can be either passive or domineering when dealing with the rest of society, but most have low self-esteem. Sadly, they really believe they know what's best for their children. The result is their children lash out against the unjust restrictions imposed on them. Some even resort to running away from home. The parent on the other hand, feels that their children don't appreciate what they're doing for them. Comments similar to, *"After all I've done for you!"* are normal responses to their children's rebellion.

Family counselling is often the only solution for this kind of obsession. Hopefully, you'll get it soon, before you and your husband lose your children's respect and co-operation entirely.

Forgetful or negligent

"My husband conveniently 'forgets' things. His usual comment is, 'Sorry, I forgot.' or 'I thought you were looking after that!' Or, 'I didn't know you wanted me to stop at the store for milk!' Is he really forgetting all those things, or is this his way of manipulating himself out of doing things?"

This is passive resistant behaviour. Those who exhibit this trait, expect others to remind them of what they should do, deadlines they must meet, and who's responsible for doing what. Deal with his actions by asking him for verbal and written commitments (if necessary). This trait is especially destructive in a work situation.

Explain that it isn't your responsibility to remind him of appointments he has or activities he's supposed to attend. Give him a calendar for his own use where he can put down important dates and activities. If he asks you, *"When am I supposed to take David to his hockey practice?"* ask him to look on the calendar. If he neglected to write it down, suggest he ask his son, or call to confirm the time. Stop running interference for him. He's setting a poor role model for your children, who will pick up his bad habit and use the same tactics on others.

Too affectionate in public

"My husband insists on touching me too much in public. He's either got his arm around my waist, takes my hand or has his hand or arm on other parts of my body. My normal response is to push him away gently, which starts fights more often than not. How can I get through to him that I don't welcome his constant touching?"

The amount of touching displayed by a person often relates to the habits of their role models. His or her parents may be "touchers" and have instilled a healthy touching of each other and of their children as part of their communication process. It also could relate to his or her cultural background. In many cultures, touch is an essential part of communication, while to others, touching is an invasion of their privacy.

Your husband likely came from a background that encouraged touching. In a non-threatening way, ask him why he touches you so often. Explain how you feel when he's constantly touching you, that you feel invaded and surrounded by him and need more space. Then try to find some compromise that is acceptable to you both.

You might also consider the following: Studies show that in public, most North American men are more likely to put their arm around their partner and the women are likely to start contact by linking arms. Most men under 30 exhibit possessiveness by frequent touching. This changes in women over 30, who reverse roles; they become the more frequent touchers.

Wife is Promoted

"I've been climbing the corporate ladder rather quickly and find myself earning more than my husband. Unfortunately, he's very frustrated about the situation. He isn't open about expressing his feelings. Instead he's argumentative, snaps at the children, and our sex life is not the same. How can I get him to accept the situation?"

Power struggles can begin after the first romantic fantasy between a couple fades, and they begin seeing each other as real people. Once they begin working as a team, they have dozens of power issues to negotiate. These can be from who pays the rent to who takes out the garbage. Often a new baby, a career switch, or a move to a new city can renew a power feud.

The most trivial disagreements disguise power struggles. These include who spends money too quickly to why one is always late for dinner. Conflicts about money, sex, planning for the future, withholding information and non-commitment hide power struggles. Once you've pinpointed power conflicts in these trouble spots, you'll have to face them head on. You may notice that you're doing more than your share of the drudge work. It could be that you feel you spend too much of your weekends just working, when you'd like to be relaxing.

If you feel frustrated, angry, or shut out of the relationship, ask yourself why. There's a good chance that an underlying power struggle between you and your mate is occurring. Talk in specifics. Talk about why s/he's late, or not treating you well. It may be how rotten you feel when she ignores you, how shut out you feel when he never tells you what he's thinking etc. Unless you resolve these power issues, the two-some, might revert to a one-some. Keep communication lines open. Use feedback to resolve these issues.

Sarcastic comments

"My husband is very sarcastic. He and his buddies are always seeing who can one-up the other with their sarcastic remarks. I don't care if they use it among themselves, but I find he's also using it on me and our children. The other day our son ended up crying because of his sarcasm. How can I make him see how cruel his comments are to the receiver?"

There are two basic kinds of sarcasm. Some sarcasm is nothing more than harmless kidding that is humorous for all concerned. Many comedians use it, as do good friends. It's non-threatening because the speakers make fun of themselves or situations. They do not use it to put others down.

Strong laughter at a joke can relieve headaches and lower a person's blood pressure and create bonds between people. The urge to share a joke of this kind is almost irresistible.

The second kind is hurtful, and designed to make others feel small. This kind of sarcasm is a form of indirect aggression. People using it feel a sense of power at seeing other people squirm, by pointing out and laughing at others' shortcomings. Because their jest is often subtle and open to more than one interpretation, it can be used to communicate taboo interests and values, to probe for what the other person is thinking, or to make a suggestion the joker is not sure will be accepted. Through their joking comments, they can mention forbidden subjects, engage in offensive or childish behaviour and even step out of the bounds of good taste.

These people resort to the hurting kind of sarcasm to express negative emotions. They're usually reluctant to confront the cause of their sarcastic remarks directly. They accomplish this through pranks, ridicule or jokes at someone else's expense. Examples of conversations using hurting sarcasm are:

"You finally decided to honour us with your presence."
"You're not exactly Mr. Efficiency yourself."
"If you're so smart, why aren't you my boss?"

You've just tipped over a cup of coffee. Comment, *"You didn't miss any of us with your coffee this time did you!"*

You ask a person to repeat a comment. They reply, *"Is English your second language?"*

It's no longer acceptable in society for people to hit others. So now they use cutting words (sarcasm) to accomplish this end. Hurtful sarcasm is one of the sneakiest, most manipulative and underhanded methods of getting one's way.

Men and women view and use sarcasm differently. Men are much harder on each other. For example: Men are often very sensitive about baldness. When buddies notice a small bald patch on the head of one of their buddies, his new nick name becomes, "Baldy."

Consider what would happen if a woman used this kind of sarcasm on another woman. For instance: Can you really picture one woman saying to another, *"How are you doing today, flabby thighs?"* It's likely that the other woman would never speak to her again!

Women who grew up with brothers who used this form of sarcasm have an advantage. Women who have not been privy to it however, react as if the man hit them if he uses men's hard type of sarcasm on them. In some ways, they have hit them -verbally, and few women really know how to deal with it. Many will act hurt and defensive. The sarcastic man's reaction to the woman's behaviour is often, *"Can't you take a joke?"* Women should ask the giver of the sarcasm to explain the "joke" to them.

It's important that we look behind the reasons people use the hurting, cutting kind of sarcasm. It's because it makes THEM feel more important. Emotionally, they don't feel very good about themselves, so they put others down to make themselves feel more important. The game continues when others respond defensively or act hurt, and are happiest when others get angry and defend themselves. Remind yourself not to respond negatively to their remarks. Try to stick to the facts. Think for a minute: who's in control in this situation? You are (the recipient of the sarcasm). Should you respond to sarcasm with more sarcasm? No, otherwise you relinquish your control of the situation, and it seldom does anything to stop the barrage, (and often encourages more of the same). Instead, analyze why they might feel so inferior that they have to put you down to feel good about themselves. Are you smarter, better looking, do your

93

job better, your supervisor likes you better -what is it? Once you have an idea of what it is, you can feel sorry for them, rather than get angry. Then you can deal with the real issue.

When you might never see the person again, simply don't react to sarcasm - instead, turn it off or ignore it. Because it's no longer fun to throw sarcasm at you, the're likely to take their sarcastic remarks elsewhere.

If you can't stay quiet, or you're having to deal with the person regularly, you may feel their actions warrant an answer. You could state, *"Your last comment was very sarcastic, and a put-down. Put-downs hurt. Can you explain why you said what you did?"* Or,

"Why did you feel the need to give me a put down like that?"

Make aggressive people account for their actions. Often they may not be aware of how destructive their behaviour is to others.

Another approach to sarcasm is to say, *"That was very sarcastic. What is it that you really wanted to say to me that you're covering up with sarcasm?"* This should at least cause the person to analyze why they made the remark, and what they really meant to say with their remarks.

In your son's case, he needs you to point out to your husband how cruel his comments are. His comments are a form of emotional abuse aimed at his vulnerable children who have few ways of fighting such comments. If the child has done something to upset him, he should correct the behaviour, not throw low blows at the child that will affect his self-esteem level.

Hopefully, you don't retaliate and use this kind of sarcasm. If you see yourself using this negative behaviour, work on being more direct during your communication with people.

Emotional Abuse

Either spouse can suffer from emotional abuse occasionally or continually. True emotional abuse involves a *constant* deluge of intimidating, sarcastic remarks, demanding, reprimanding, blaming, shouting, belittling, or emotional blackmail.

Emotional blackmail occurs when the abuser plays on the person's fear, guilt or compassion. A familiar comment from the abuser is *"Look at what you've made me do!"* They search for someone to blame for all their negative emotions. When things go wrong in their life, it's always someone else's fault. As you've learned earlier in this book - everyone is responsible for their own emotions - they can't blame others for how they feel or react.

Abusers constantly depreciate the person's self-esteem and self-confidence levels, can be very unpredictable and prone to drastic mood swings. For example:

Friends of Sandra and Ben have seen drastic changes in them since their marriage a year ago. Sandra had been a bubbly, outgoing woman who desperately loved Ben and went out of her way to please him. Ben was very proud of his beautiful, successful wife and bragged about her to everyone.

By the end of their first year of marriage, she became a quiet, apologetic person who tried so hard to please, that she gave up most of the activities she liked to do before her marriage. She slowly dropped all her old friends and became more and more withdrawn.

Ben changed from being a polite, easy-going man, into one who became openly manipulative, belittling and judgemental of Sandra's accomplishments.

The signs were there - their marriage had become an emotionally abusive relationship. The abuse started slowly and gained momentum over time.

Although it can be women emotionally abusing men, most victims of emotional abuse are women who believe they're responsible for their partner's or others' happiness and well-being. She believes her job is to fix relationships, and she feels guilty if she can't.

More often than not, children in these relationships, are also emotionally abused. They in turn, follow their role models and repeat the cycle in the next generation. Society needs to identify the signs of abuse and take steps to help the abuser change by providing counselling to the abused so he or she will get out of the destructive relationship and stop the cycle from repeating itself.

Workaholic Husband

"My husband has been a workaholic for years, but the situation's getting worse. Our children and I never see him any more, and he's always tired. There's no need for him to work as hard as he does. We could manage on much less financially than we do now, but he won't listen to me when I tell him this. What causes him to work so hard, and why won't he listen to me when I tell him what's happening to our family?"

Most people assume that workaholics are unhappy, but that's not always true. There are three kinds of workaholics:

* Those who work because they truly love to work - love their jobs - work hard and long because they receive pleasure from doing so. They're under stress but seldom suffer from distress.
* Those who are motivated not by enthusiasm but by such things as:
  - competitive feelings
  - job pressures
  - budget cuts
  - family or relationship problems
  - financial problems
* Those who work because they feel driven to do so (compulsive behaviour). Their stress becomes distress and they suffer because of it.

It sounds as if your husband fits into the third group. These workaholics normally have the following characteristics:
* They fear failure.
* They fear being thought of as lazy.
* They fear others will find out that they aren't as good as they think they are, or they're slipping in their ability level.

Workaholism signs

We all know the people in the second and third categories. They:

* are always working, often bringing home work in the evening and on the weekend - but are resentful about it.
* suffer from nervous disorders.
* don't eat or exercise right.
* seldom spend time with their family.
* never take time off from work when they're ill. (They're the ones who pass on the flu bug to the rest of the staff because they <u>do</u> come in when they shouldn't.)
* don't know how to relax, to play or simply "goof-off."

(They often use competitive sports to relax.) They're willing to take risks when they feel secure, but when things pile up, they fall back to dealing with stress the way they always have. Many of these ways are destructive. The hard working person becomes a workaholic, others drink, overeat, take drugs or have other compulsions.

Some workaholics are addicts who use work as their drug of choice. They can be emotional cripples wired into power and control. Obsession drives them in their often fruitless search for perfection, approval and success. They're always running, always busy - even when they're on vacation. This driving force often results in heart trouble, shaking, nervousness, stomach upsets, trouble breathing, dizziness and light-headedness.

Have a serious talk with your husband. Don't let him leave your talk without explaining why he's working so hard and the effect it is having on his family. A very simple question to ask him, which might shock him into realistically looking at what he's doing is, *"Suppose our doctor told you that you had only six months to live. What would you be doing during that six months?"*

He likely would say that he'd spend more time with his family, travel or something other than working hard. This reality check might jump-start him on the road to changing his priorities. If that doesn't work, you may have to identify some of the consequences that could happen should his behaviour not change (be ready for this *before* your meeting. Marriage counselling might be warranted especially if he admits that he's working to get away from his family situation.

Workaholics can obtain more help by reading the book: *"Workaholics - the Respectable Addicts"*, by Dr. Barbara Killinger. See Chapter 7 to learn about burnout.

Husband loses job

"My husband Bill lost his job three months ago. Not only has this created financial problems, but it has been emotionally draining on us both. I too have experienced fear, insecurity, shock, and anger. How can I help him when I'm overwhelmed by my own emotions?"

The stresses of job termination can create as much hurt and confusion for the spouse as for the person losing the job. Some husbands withdraw and won't discuss their problems because they're ashamed or feel they've let their family down. Their wives feel hurt and isolated by their husband's reaction to the blow to his self-esteem.

One excellent source of help in this area is the book, *"I've Been Fired Too: Coping with your Husband's Job Loss."* by Jill Jukes and Ruthan Rosenberg.

Snoring

"My husband snores so loudly that I can't even be on the same floor as he is, let alone sleep in the same bed as he does. This still doesn't give me a good sleep because I keep reading about sleep apnoea and the danger he might be in if he has it. What can I do to make him realize that we have a serious problem."

Take heart - snoring has noble origins that go back to prehistoric days. For those who have to put up with snorers, this knowledge probably won't make up for the hours of sleep they've missed. Nor will it make up to the snorers who've been elbowed, yelled at and even kicked out of their own beds.

A recent study suggests that we shouldn't hit a snoring man, because:

a) He might hit back!
b) In his own way he may be protecting you!

That roof-jarring commotion may be the remains of an ancient protective device that's outlived its use. Some believe that male hormones may be the culprit, for men snore far more, and far louder than most women. In addition, snoring occurs during a person's period of deepest sleep, when their conscious mind is least aware of its surroundings and when the snorer is most vulnerable.

But pray tell, why do men snore so much louder than women? Well, there is an explanation. When our human ancestors left the safety of the jungle and ventured onto the materializing tundra some five million years ago, sleep proved to be one of man's most defenceless times of the day. So nature stepped in, and provided men with a unique defense mechanism. It enabled men to utter the earth-shattering noises they practice nightly. By mimicking the sounds of their most common predators (the carnivorous nocturnal cats and hyenas), early man could broadcast throughout the night: "Hear me roar! Leave us alone or you'll have to contend with a mighty warrior!"

That knowledge probably isn't going to help modern men and women (except to give them a chuckle or two). So what is one to do to stop the din and bring peace to homes once again? Many resort to unusual treatments such as taping a tennis ball between the snorer's shoulder blades. Others give a sharp elbow to shock the person into retreating from the offensive object. Some resort to taping their mouths so they can't breathe through their mouths. Some resort to sleeping sitting up by piling up to six pillows behind them. Most of these remedies provide only temporary relief.

Then what works? Start with a thorough medical. People who snore usually do so because there's an obstruction to the free flow of air in their breathing passages, often caused by excessive tissue in the uvula and soft palate near their throat. A new laser treatment can eliminate snoring in most patients by using a technique that burns away tissue in the passages at the back of the mouth and nose, reshaping and reforming the opening which allows for greater airflow. After three to five 10-minute office visits under local anaesthesia, 85 to 90 per cent of patients given the laser treatment stop snoring. Most find the treatment an almost painless process.

Far more serious than the snoring itself is "sleep apnoea" which occasionally accompanies snoring. Often, this distinct, rhythmic form of snoring (four or five times in quick succession, then a 20- to 40- second pause, then a new eruption) results from a blockage of the snorer's air passages. This can occur if the person's tongue falls back in the mouth and their throat muscles relax. They lack the ability to sleep and breathe regularly at the same time.

Their snores are actually the brain rousing itself so their body is stimulated to gasp for air.

People with short, receding jaws are prone to this condition. Many sufferers have fat necks that narrow the throat passages further. The first treatment prescribed in those cases is weight loss. There are also medications that promote regular breathing, and small nasal masks work with some patients. Put on at bedtime, the mask is connected by a tube to a miniature blower that forces air into the nose to keep breathing passages open.

A simple operation to cut away tissue lining at the back of the throat, remedies most cases. Extreme cases, however may require a tracheotomy. (If you snore constantly, or snore and feel good in the morning, you probably don't have apnoea.)

CHAPTER 7
DIFFICULT WIVES

This chapter concentrates on problems husbands have with their wives.

Dependent

"My wife is smothering me! She's so dependent on me that it's making me want to stay away from our home. She waits all day for me to come home, and monopolizes my time so much that I have no privacy at all. I've told her repeatedly that she's smothering me, and have asked her for some 'space,' but she won't listen to me. What do I have to do, threaten to leave her before she hears me?"

This is a form of passive behaviour. Dependent people believe that they should be dependent on others and must have someone stronger on whom to rely. Dependency causes greater dependency, failure to learn, and insecurity, since one is at the mercy of those on whom one depends.

Most dependent adults grew up in homes where the parents taught their children to be dependent and to lean on them. Women from these homes usually switch their dependency to their husbands when they marry. This is an almost automatic response. If she had lived on her own before her marriage, she would likely have lost her dependent nature.

Your wife needs encouragement from you to see that she has an independent life of her own. Unfortunately, she went right from her parents home into your marriage. Her passive behaviour keeps her from attempting independent action. Try sending her to assertiveness training course, or buy her some books on the topic. You might suggest that she get a job outside the home to help her make independent decisions.

Encourage her to refuse help unless it's necessary. Help her know that risks - while possibly resulting in failures - are worth taking, and failing is not a catastrophe.

When she asks you for help in deciding - stop yourself from doing so. Instead ask her, *"What do you think you should do?"* Nine times out of ten, she'll know what she should do - she just wants confirmation. When she realizes that she knew what to do all along, she'll see that she can make more decisions by herself.

Driving problems

"My wife Marianne is always giving me advice when I'm driving. She drives me to distraction with her interference. 'How come you took this route to the football game?' Or, 'Why don't you plan your route better - it takes you twice as long to get where we're going.'"

Your wife likes to be in control. When you're driving, she's not in control. One comment you might make, is, *"Who's driving? If you have so many complaints about my driving, you can drive the next time. Meanwhile, I don't want to hear any more complaints about my driving."* If she persists, pull over to the side of the road (safely) and ask her to drive. If necessary, quit driving if she's going to be a passenger.

Have you tried to analyze why she chooses times when you're in the car to criticize you? She may suffer from anxiety when she travels in a car.

"My husband insists on driving over the speed limit. Not only am I afraid that he'll get a ticket, but I feel he's dangerous to everyone on the road when he drives so fast. His explanation is, 'Everyone else drives over the speed limit. Police never enforce posted speed limits. They allow me to go 10 kilometres over the speed limit before they even care.'"

Most serious car accidents involving serious injury and/or death, are caused by those who are either intoxicated or driving over the speed limit. His explanation doesn't hold water.

Because this involves the issue of values, you'll have to decide whether you and your children will continue being with him when he's driving. Explain your dislike of his obvious disrespect for the law, and lack of concern about his own safety and that of others. This might cause serious repercussions in your marriage. You may need marriage counselling to resolve this serious, but potentially life threatening problem.

Financial problems

"My wife and I have two children. We both work because it's a financial necessity. She knows this, but she's often absent from work because of one reason or another. She hates her job, and finds all kinds of excuses to stay away. I'm afraid she may lose her job, and this has caused many arguments lately."

The average women these days, spends 35 years of her adult life in the workplace, working either part- or full-time. So, if she's in a job she dislikes, just think of how many more years she's likely to hate her work before she retires. Encourage her to speak to a career specialist and get career counselling (this is a free government service in many centres). They'll help her identify her transferable skills and suggest alternate occupations where she can use those skills.

It's also possible, that your wife's not getting enough help around the home. A family conference is in order (see Chapter 10) to ensure that she doesn't have too many home responsibilities.

Stealing from work

"My wife Cheryl works in an office. She occasionally brings paperclips, pens, felts, lined paper, and staples home from work. Our children have watched and commented on her stealing. I know I've got to talk to my wife about her stealing from work. What should I say to her that won't sound like preaching?"

Explain how you feel about it. For Instance, *"Cheryl, I need to talk to you today, because something concerns me. I watched Judy the other day when you came home from work with some lined paper. This afternoon, she asked me if it was okay to take items from school the way you take some from work. I suggested she talk to you about this when you come home. I wanted to warn you about this before she approaches you. You probably haven't realized how she perceives what you're doing. She wants to know if it's all right to steal - because that's exactly what this is. How do you think you'll approach this?"*

This will prepare Cheryl for the situation and make her look closely at the example she's setting for your children. Between you, decide a rational course of action and what she should tell your children about what she's been doing.

Saboteur

"My wife Jane's community club appointed her to make coffee for the participants at their meetings. She hates making coffee, but rather than admit her reluctance, she sabotages and makes lousy coffee. Once she uses half a package of coffee, then one and a half packages in the hope that they will appoint someone else to do the job. She did this, until a member of the committee asked her whether she would prefer to swap tasks with another committee member. How can I make her see that she should be more direct, instead of sabotaging tasks she doesn't want to do?"

The saboteur goes through the motions, but fights the situation every step of the way. This is another form of passive resistance. This behaviour in adults, just makes them look very childish and inept. Many children act this way when parents delegate a distasteful task such as taking out the garbage. Their parents often have to face a trail of garbage down the sidewalk to the outer garbage can. The child believes that if she or he does a bad enough job, someone else will have it delegated to them.

Adults are no different. Those who sabotage tasks should suffer the consequences of their actions. They should do the task until they do it correctly.

In your wife's case, encourage her to be more honest with others. If she dislikes a task, she should say so instead of using manipulative behaviour to get out of doing the task. She may need to attend assertiveness training classes to learn that manipulating others is not as effective as being direct with them.

Smoking Problem

"Every time my wife Jessie lights up a cigarette, our thirteen-year-old daughter Kyla starts up with, 'You're not only killing yourself, but you're killing us too. ' She's parroting what they're saying at her school, which has made her feel concerned for her own health as well.

I, too find that the smell from her clothing and hair is affecting our sex life. She smells like an ashtray and it turns me right off. We're hoping to have another child so smoking causes many battles in our home. Jessie can't quit for longer than a month at a time. I quit myself, six years ago when I developed a cough. What can I do to get a truce and get some peace around my home?"

Family fights over smoking are virulent and often bitter. Other than having patience and showing your understanding of both sides of the issue, you can try to influence her with the following information that has been released by the American Lung Association:

- Children who live in households with adult smokers are more likely to be in worse health than those in smoke-free homes.
- Coughing isn't the only health problem smokers force on their children. The polluted indoor air causes 30 per cent more lower-respiratory problems in children whose parents smoke than in non-smoking families.
- Children of parents who smoke, receive hospitalization more frequently for bronchitis and pneumonia during the first year of life compared with the children of non-smokers. Second-hand smoke also causes eye and sinus irritation.
- Pregnant women who smoke are more likely to have babies who are underweight, born prematurely, die in their first year or have breathing and heart problems. About 25 per cent of all pregnant American women smoke throughout their pregnancies. About 30 per cent of women who smoke, quit when they find out they're pregnant. Unfortunately, during the interim, the baby has been exposed to the mother's smoke during it's most important developmental stage.

Another health bulletin states *"Cigarette smoke may cause a catastrophic disruption of the chromosomes in human eggs that can lead to miscarriage. Women who smoke produce some immature eggs that produce highly abnormal fetuses that nearly always result in miscarriages. "*

Encourage her to stop smoking, remembering that it could be a very difficult sacrifice. Suggest she determine a substantial reward she can give herself if she's successful in stopping for one year. Have her decide how much she would have paid for cigarettes during that year. You might suggest a second honeymoon in Hawaii (if that would tempt her).

If she can't stop, at least ask her to smoke outside the home. Putting aside one room in the home for smoking doesn't work because the smoke permeates the rest of the home eventually.

Burnout

"My wife is a nervous wreck. She is very dedicated to her job and is a wonderful wife and mother. She helps her elderly parents shop every weekend, but seldom has any free time for herself. I'm worried about her, but don't know how to get her to slow down. Is she headed for burnout?"

Ask your wife to read the section in Chapter 6 about workaholism. If her workaholism and stress keep up long enough, the almost inevitable result will be "burnout" (formerly called a nervous breakdown). To check for signs of burnout, talk to her and ask her the following questions:

Do You:
--feel down or depressed most of the time?
--have trouble eating and sleeping properly?
--feel there's no hope for improvement in your circumstances?
--complain constantly?
--feel that no one cares?
--experience feelings of intense pressure and competition at
    work?
--feel that no matter what you do it won't be enough?
--fear that you're going under any day now?

If she feels even two or three of these, she could be in trouble. Help her identify activities she can drop or delegate to someone else. It's not likely she can reduce her work stress unless she can work fewer hours. Could you or your children help more at home? Could anyone else step in and help with her parents? Families that work together as a team can be a great help to those approaching burnout. See that the situation does not repeat itself in the future because workaholics tend to revert to old behaviours.

Heart Problems

"Last month my wife had a heart attack. She's home from the hospital now, but I find I don't sleep well at night. I haven't talked to her about it, but I'm afraid that I'll wake up some morning and find her dead in the bed beside me."

This is understandable in the circumstances. Speak to her doctor to see how she's really doing and whether your fears are warranted. Take a CPR (coronary pulmonary resuscitation) course so you can act if she has another heart attack. Then if necessary, you can do your best to revive her.

If your wife is alone for a long time, get her an alert system that she wears around her neck that can summon help in seconds. This will not only make you feel better, but will make her feel as if she has more control should there be another emergency.

Wife has PMS

"My wife's having a terrible time. For years she's felt bloated, has aches, and mood swings. She finally had her problem diagnosed as pre-menstrual tension. How can I help her through this?"

Women who suffer from PMS (pre-menstrual tension) not only have terrible pain, but suffer from emotional symptoms that many describe as, *"I thought I was going out of my mind! I yelled . . . I screamed . . . I ranted and raved!"* They're very frightened women because they're afraid their wild mood swings are going to end their marriages, or they're going to harm their children.

Because little research had been done on women's problems, women in the 60's and early 70's were treated with tranquilizers (as if it was a mental illness, not a hormonal illness). This just enhanced the women's belief that they WERE mentally ill and their husbands couldn't help wondering whether they had married someone with a mental illness.

Modern medicine has come a long way in treating this female malady. Now, doctors realize PMS happens because a woman's estrogen level is very high. According to specialists, they can eliminate the severest form of PMS by stopping ovulation by drugs, by pregnancy and by menopause. Doctors encourage all sufferers to learn stress relieving techniques and relaxation methods, and can prescribe synthetic steroids that stop menstruation in extreme cases. There are four basic types of PMS:

A. Type: Anxiety
B. Type: Fluid retention
C. Type: Food cravings
D. Type: Depression

Many women suffer from these symptoms either moderately or severely. More than 90 per cent of women are likely to suffer from a mild variety that they notice, but don't believe affects their lifestyle. These women learn to exercise more, use less salt, sugar and caffeine and take vitamin B6.

The moderate type, interferes with the woman's lifestyle, but isn't incapacitating. These women watch the calendar and try to rearrange events to suit their menstrual cycle. They receive treatment to balance their estrogen-progesterone relationship.

The severest type of PMS is disabling. Some women are prone to deep depression and can become violent and feel suicidal.

Wife Sexually Harassed at Work

"My wife came home the other day very upset, and crying. I spent the evening trying to find out what had happened to her at work. At first she said, 'I'll handle it.' But as the evening progressed, she still didn't settle down. I insisted that she tell me what was wrong.

'I'm being sexually harassed at work!' she exclaimed.

My first thought was to go to work with her the next day and 'punch the man's lights out!'

'That's what I was afraid you'd want to do! What I need are solutions to the problem, not more problems to worry about. That's why I didn't want to tell you about this in the first place.'.

With that, we sat down and wrote down the alternatives open to her. I wanted her to quit her job the next day, but she was adamant that she loved her job, and nobody was going to force her to leave it.

We decided that the best alternative would be to call the Human Right's commission in our area to find out what her rights were, and how to handle her situation. Meanwhile, my wife called her office and said she was ill (she really couldn't work that day).

The Human Rights Commission advised us that she should document everything that happened, try to find witnesses to the actions, and whether this man had harassed other women in her company. She was to send copies of this documentation to the man who harassed her, her supervisor and his manager. By law, she could charge these people with sexual harassment especially if the man didn't stop harassing her. Those in senior positions couldn't 'turn the other cheek' and ignore her plight, otherwise she could charge them with harassment as well. Their silence would mean they condoned the sexual harassment. Because of their senior positions, they should have stepped in and done something to stop the harassment.

We followed their advice, she confronted the man, and got an assurance from him that he would not harass my wife in the future."

In an article about Gloria Steinem, (January 1992, Working Woman) she put this issue into the right perspective. She related to the reality that rape is not about sex, but violence; sexual harassment is not about sex, but about power; pornography is not about sex, but about violence. Her comments relating to the Anita Hill-Clarence Thomas hearings on sexual harassment hit home with me: "I think people were also quite moved in some way by Thomas's portrayal of himself and by his anger, which scares people. He was very scary. I was thinking of writing an open letter to him and saying - you know, this is my optimistic self - Whether or not the charges are true, you have sat in a room with 14 men speculating on your sex life, on parts of your anatomy, for days and days and days. Now you know what women in the work force go through every day."

I discuss sexual harassment at several of my seminars by explaining what sexual harassment is, what victims can do about it, and where they can go to complain formally. Sexual harassment can be:

Verbal:
* telling dirty jokes with sexual connotations
* asking for sexual favours
* comments about one's sexual anatomy
* pursuing an unwanted relationship
* unwanted compliments with sexual overtones
* condescension or paternalism that undermines self-respect

Visual:
* staring at someone's sexual anatomy
* holding uncomfortably long eye contact giving sexual messages
* flirting non-verbally
* pornographic pictures

Physical:
* unwanted touching and making physical contact
* standing too close

In classes where there are both male and female participants, I often receive comments such as, *"Why should men have to 'clean up their act' just because women are now working in a male-dominated field? They're the ones invading our turf so they should have to abide by our rules, not theirs!"*

My normal response to this comment is, *"I know it's difficult to change your conversational patterns because of this change in the workplace. I'd like to ask all of you who object to cleaning up your language, whether you use this type of language at home?"* Most agree that they don't use that kind of language at home. *"Then why do you think it's acceptable in a professional place of business?"*

My next question to them is, *"Do any of you have daughters and how old are they?"* Usually a few hands go up. To those, I ask, *"When they're old enough to work, say seventeen, what would you do if you learned that someone she works with was sexually harassing her? What would you do if it was your sister, girlfriend, wife or mother being harassed?"*

A common answer is, *"I'd punch his lights out!"* My next comment is, *"Let's turn this around. How do you think the boyfriends, husbands and fathers of the women you're sexually harassing feel about your actions? Why do you feel it's acceptable to treat any women that way?"*

This usually puts the situation into a clearer light. They suddenly realize that if they'd like to *"punch someone's lights out"* if someone harassed their wife, sweetheart or daughter, then maybe the female they're harassing has a father, husband or boyfriend who might be thinking about doing the very same thing to them!

Sexual harassment can be a man harassing a woman (the most common complaint) a woman harassing a man, a man harassing another man, or a woman harassing another woman. For example, if I tell offensive jokes and refuse to stop telling them, another woman could charge me with sexual harassment (female charging another female). The same holds true of a male co-worker who can also charge me with sexual harassment if he objects to my lewd jokes (male charging a female).

Death of wife

"My wife died suddenly in a car accident. Not only am I having a terrible time getting through this, but my children are too. How can I help them?"

Children who've had a parent die may go into shock. Some deny that their parent is dead or lack signs that express grief. Treat these danger signals immediately. Like adults, children must grieve. Could they feel guilty, possibly because of words they may have exchanged with to their mother before she died? Could they feel somewhat responsible for her death?

How are they doing at school? Warn the school authorities about the mother's death and ask them to keep you informed about any unusual behaviour of the child. If serious problems surface, ask your clergyman or a psychologist to help you and your children deal with your grief.

111

CHAPTER 8
DEALING WITH CHILDREN

Courtesy to others

Sharing and caring for each other takes a nosedive when families stop using common courtesy and everyday manners with each other. Why don't they treat family members with the same courtesy they give to their friends or even strangers? They drift into it - because of bad habits, familiarity, and an uncaring attitude. This sets the stage for children's actions with others.

The idea, *"My family will like me no matter how I act,"* becomes their behaviour pattern. Unless they identify and correct this negative habit, it will just continue unabated. The family will likely grow apart.

Couples who stay together "because of the children" are often surprised by the reaction of their children when they finally decide to separate. Their children wonder why their parents stayed together as long as they did.

Children, teens and young adults are strongly affected by how they see their parents treating each other. They're more upset by non-verbal expressions of anger such as sarcasm and the silent treatment than was originally thought. Children watch how their parents show their anger, and how they act after they fight. Unresolved anger bothers children, and they're very quick to pick up tension between their parents.

Children as young as nine months old sense and become distressed when their parents are fighting. Arguments that parents haven't resolved during a confrontation, sit there like time bombs, and children wait anxiously for them to erupt again.

Arguments that express anger in a physical way using hitting and pushing, are far more damaging and hard to forget for most children. They also learn that hitting and pushing during arguments are acceptable behaviour. They use this behaviour on their friends and schoolmates, which causes spin-off problems.

Children need to know that arguments have their place. Parents need to show obvious signs that an argument is solved and be willing to negotiate or compromise. Arguments that conclude with parents apologizing to each other, help children understand that all arguments aren't wrong. This kind of argument doesn't have a lasting effect on children. They learn that arguments are all right if they're solved peacefully and end with no winners or losers.

A parent's non-verbal behaviour can often be misinterpreted by children which can cause spin-off problems. Let's say Mom comes in the front door, and doesn't say *"Hi,"* like she normally does.

Her children's reaction would probably be, *"I wonder what I did wrong, that Mom isn't speaking to me?"* By her silence, the children pick up the wrong message. The parent needs to let them know that it isn't them she's mad at, but what's happened to her earlier in the day.

She might say, *"Hi guys. I've had a terrible day today, so give me a bit of time to get my act together."* She should spare her children from the belief that they've done something to annoy her.

Too much to do!

Many families have little time to spend with each other or their children. Everything piles up, and they find themselves rushed off their feet.

The answer to this is to get everyone in the household involved in getting chores done. It's not just husbands who require encouragement to help at home. Some children believe that Mom should make their beds, clear their dishes off the table and cater to their every need. Children who grow up believing that while they're children, they're on this earth to have nothing but fun, are deprived on one of life's important learning experiences.

Parents should never do for children what they can do for themselves. If they do, they only breed dependent, often demanding children who expect a "free ride" through life, and depend on external events to make them happy. These children seldom achieve the exhilarating feeling of independence that comes from knowing they can do whatever is necessary to succeed.

Couples who share parenting and household duties, cope better than couples who follow traditional practices. Their children become part of the "team," become responsible for their actions, and take part in the smooth running of the home.

Both parents can help make this happen. They're encouraged to:

--Spend individual time with each child that the child thinks of as his or her "special" time with the parent (many choose bedtime as their private time with their child). This can be ten to fifteen minutes each day, and a set time on the weekend.

--Keep track of their children's "other lives"--at the baby-sitter, the day-care centre, kindergarten, school, sports and artistic activities, etc. Learn about special events at school and take time to attend. Encourage their children to keep them informed.

--Practice effective listening and try not to be judgemental. They don't make times with their children an inquisition. They hear what their children are *not* saying by watching their body language.

--Use effective time planning to eliminate unnecessary steps and tasks to give themselves more time with their families. They establish priorities, remembering to put their children high on their list of essentials.

--Enlist their children's help, or ask for their presence when they're doing chores, so they can chat with them.

--Plan special outings that cater to individual needs. At a family conference (discussed in Chapter 10), each member states the special activities s/he likes to do as a family. Use this list when planning special outings.

--Are aware of their stress level so they don't overreact to minor incidents with their children. If they've had a bad day, they explain this to their children and ask if they can talk to them later. They don't put them off too long - follow-up promptly.

--They don't feel guilty when they need "private time," and remember to honour their children's need for privacy too. (We'll be discussing how to accomplish this in Chapter 10 as well).

Finding the right child care

Mom has decided to go back to work, either because she wants to or it's financially necessary. She's excited at the prospect of returning to work, but is anxious about the contradictory feelings of going back to work versus staying home with her children. The thought of searching for someone else to care for her children gives her cold shivers. She recalls all the horror stories in the newspaper about abusive babysitters and child molesters.

Others worry that many nannies and babysitters are from other cultures, which could complicate the upbringing of their children. What these women are really looking for, are replacements for themselves, but they're not likely to find the exact match for their needs. They must make some compromises, but never at the risk of the children's safety and well-being.

Parents need to listen to their initial instincts about a potential child-care worker. After all, these children are a couples' most precious legacy to the future. If feelings about the person are positive, checking the references for child-care workers is still a must. If everything is in order - they should hire the person. If anything is questionable, they should listen to their instincts and look elsewhere. Many parents unfortunately don't listen to their instinctive responses, and serious problems are the result.

Negative tapes

When children are young, they depend on their care-givers to either make them feel good or bad about themselves. Most parents and caregivers are loving and want everything to go well. Unfortunately, some caregivers don't realize what destructive criticism can do to the fragile ego of a child. People hear and perceive exactly what they want to hear based on their earlier experiences, values, and biases.

Children's self-esteem level is strongly influenced by how they are criticized. Constructive criticism talks about a child's behaviour. Destructive criticism on the other hand, is exactly that - destructive. It eats away at the psyche of the child until they lose their self-respect.

One form of destructive criticism is to label the child. For example, *"Benny, you're the most sloppy child I know."* That's labelling Benny and is a form of emotional abuse.

"Benny, that's the third time you've spilled your milk!" This discusses Benny's behaviour. Benny can change his behaviour, but doesn't really understand how he can stop being sloppy, careless, dumb, or stupid.

If you catch yourself labelling anyone, apologize immediately. Say, *"I'm sorry, you didn't deserve that remark. What I meant to say was . . . "* Then discuss the behaviour that offended you.

Many parents have labelled children so often that the children grow up with "negative tapes" that replay throughout their adult lives. Many never rid themselves of these negative tapes. Here are examples of constructive and destructive criticism:

Destructive criticism	Constructive Criticism
- "You're not as smart as your brother are you?"	- "You really excel at sports. Could you try a little harder to get better grades?"
- "Can't you do anything right?"	- "You know you can do better than this. Look at how well you did on your last test."
- "What a clutz you are, that's three times you've done that wrong."	- "You seem to be having trouble with this project. Can I help you?"

117

Destructive criticism	Constructive Criticism
- "You ought to know better."	- "Jim, you're far too old to be pulling stunts like that. Can you tell me why you're doing this?"
- "You're a naughty girl."	- "Jill don't write on the wall!"
- "You're a bad boy."	- "Billy, I've just cleaned the house. Please pick up your belongings and put them away."
- "You're so inconsiderate!"	- "I won't allow that kind of behaviour. Please apologize to Bob for not sharing the toys."
- "Jenny, you're the sloppiest child I know!"	- "Jenny, please try to be more careful with your paint set. They leave stains when you spill them."
- "Sometimes I wish I'd never had kids."	- "You've been very noisy this afternoon. Please go to your room so you can have some quiet time before dinner."
- "Mary, this is a "D." How dumb can you be?"	- "Let's talk about your report card Mary. I'm concerned about the "D" you got in math."
- "Must you always look like such a slob?"	- "Lennie, please go back to your room and put on a clean shirt."
- "What a spoiled brat you are!"	- "Jimmy, you're not to throw toys in the house."

These destructive criticism messages are all put-downs and are almost impossible for the child to deal with. They're coming from a person in a position of power. This (as should be expected) puts the child on the defensive and gives them negative feelings about themselves. Most of these comments label the child and give them guilt feelings for not being what the powerful adults want them to be.

Labels are very destructive. For instance, how can Jenny "unbad" herself? Because the parent hasn't defined the specific behaviour Jenny's used, she really doesn't know how to start improving herself. Jenny's parents have put negative tapes in her head that may stay there until she's mature enough to realize the tapes are no longer true. But look at the damage that it's done to Jenny in the meantime!

If you feel that children are receiving negative tapes from other authority figures, step in immediately to correct the problem. All parents should occasionally sit in during their children's classes to detect whether their teachers are using labels to criticize their students. If they identify destructive criticism, the parents should speak to the teacher, and if necessary to the principal of the school.

Watch for the kind of criticism given by babysitters and day care workers. Correct your children if you catch them criticizing others improperly.

Use this information if you're criticizing adults. If you've criticized an adult and labelled them "dumb," this might confirm old negative tapes that they *are* dumb. This adds fuel to their belief that what you say is gospel. When correcting others (whether it be your children, someone else's, or an adult) it's important to consider whether you're giving them a label or discussing their behaviour.

If someone tries to give you a negative label (dumb, stupid, ignorant) instead of criticizing exactly what you've done, ask for specifics. If necessary, discuss the label they're trying to give you. Remember you have the choice of accepting or not accepting the criticism they're trying to give you.

I cover how to deal with negative tapes in one of my seminars. I noticed that one of my participants was writing madly with a wide grin on his face after I had described how destructive negative tapes could be. He was a well-dressed man about thirty-five years of age, who appeared to have his "act" together. He asked to speak to me after my class and related his story to me.

When he was thirteen, he went through the growth spurt most adolescent boys do, but he grew six inches in six months! This of course, made him a very awkward teenager. He could have survived this, except that his family, his friends, his peers at school, his teachers and even his gym instructor kept labelling him. They described him as "clumsy, clutzy awkward, uncoordinated, bumbling and lacking in dexterity." He heard these statements so often that even HE began to believe the labels.

When he was fifteen, he was six feet three inches tall; a perfect candidate for basketball. But did he try basketball? No, because he believed he was awkward, and lacked manual dexterity . . .

When it came time to learn how to dance with a girl, did he try? No, because he was clumsy, awkward . . . When he tried to fix cars, did he succeed? No, because in his mind, he was clumsy, awkward . . .

At my seminar, he'd been busy writing down all the activities he was going to try for the first time (this was the reason for the smile). As he said, *"I've wasted twenty-two years of my life thinking I couldn't do things without even trying them out. It's time for me to try them all. The first item on my list is to learn how to play basketball!"* He proved that it's never too late to change.

How much better it would have been if others had given him constructive criticism when he was a child.

Disciplining when angry

Unfortunately, parents make comments in the heat of the moment, little realizing that their negative comments can be "locked-in" for part or all their child's life. If you find you do this automatically with your child, try the following:

a. Don't speak on impulse. Walk away for a minute or take yourself away mentally for a moment, and think of something other than the problem. Count to ten.

b. Develop responses to familiar problems and strive to use them. If the child balks, consider giving firm consequences should s/he not do what you ask him or her to do and make sure you follow-through with action.

c. Concentrate on your child's positive behaviour. Most children want to please, but if the only way they perceive they can get your attention is to be bad, that's what you'll get from them. Try talking calmly about the situation. If that doesn't work, (rather than yelling or hitting them), give them isolation for their bad behaviour or start removing privileges.

d. Use humour whenever possible to control your anger. For example, picture yourself tossing an imaginary cream pie in your child's face if s/he does something to make you angry. This will defuse your anger and keep your objectivity.

e. Don't over-react, by saying or doing something you'll regret. For instance, think of when children trip, fall down, and brake something. Yelling at them for breaking the item is double punishment if they hurt themselves when they fell.

To spank or not to spank?

Spanking is a swat on the child's bottom; hitting anywhere else is considered abusive. Have you ever spanked your child? Would you admit to it, if you had?

For five decades, child-rearing professionals have preached against spanking for discipline. Not only does it hurt, but it also starts negative psychological effects and can be a forerunner to child abuse. One or two spankings in childhood are not going to be damaging, but it's hard to know the limit between discipline and abuse.

The purpose of discipline is not simply to punish, but to teach. Spanking only punishes, and seldom teaches. Spanking stops unwanted action but works only because of the child's fear and loss of trust in the spanker. A child who gets a spanking (no matter how light) can become too upset to hear what parents say. Physical punishment undermines anything else the parent might do, however positive.

If children see their parents are out of control, they seldom learn self-control themselves and lash out at others physically. Children who receive frequent spankings are more aggressive throughout their lives. They often become child bullies and adult criminals.

The worst kind of spanking involves the use of some type of tool, be it a wooden spoon, belt or a hairbrush. When parents are angry, think of what that angry, contorted face looks like to a two-year-old. It would stop most adults in their tracks. Children can't help believe that people who are bigger than they, can get away with physical aggression.

Then how do you deal with bratty, defiant and downright frustrating children? There are alternatives to spanking. Any form of discipline that breaks the cycle of unacceptable behaviour is preferable to spanking. One is the use of warnings, but make sure you follow-through with what you say you're going to do should they misbehave.

Instead of saying repeatedly, *"Johnny, if you do that again I'll . . . "* Instead, use the feedback technique described in chapter 3.

Another method of punishment is isolation. The child has misbehaved, so the parent says, *"I don't want to talk to you any more."* Most children hate isolation. Little do parents realize that the pre-school child feels frightened by this perceived abandonment by their parent. Their silent treatment is very cruel punishment.

Instead, the parent would be wise to send the child to his or her room with the comment, *"When you're ready to behave properly, you can come out of your room."* This gives the control of the isolation to the child without him or her having to suffer from the terrifying sense of abandonment.

Make sure the punishment is worse than the original situation. For instance, remove all toys from the child's room so s/he's not playing during punishment.

Punishment for young children needs to be consistent and immediate. Make sure the child knows how s/he stepped over the limits and that the punishment is the consequence. The simple understanding of cause and effect (consequences) is one of the most important concepts children can learn. The sooner children learn this philosophy, the less trouble there will be as they grow up.

For many children, a stern tone or a raised eyebrow is sufficient after they've learned to trust their parents and know that punishment for bad behaviour will be fair.

Parents may find problems occur after they find it necessary to discipline their child. After the discipline, they may want to make sure their children know they still love them, even if they have misbehaved. They try to express their feelings by hugging their children, but often the children pull away and won't let their parents touch them. This can result in a defensive reaction in the parents. They need to be patient because later, the children will likely allow hugs. The parents should watch for non-verbal signs of acceptance from their children that s/he wants comforting. The child may show this by simply re-entering the room where the parents are sitting.

Touching Children

Some children are born unusually sensitive to touch. They don't see a hug as comforting. Instead they find embraces too hot and others' arms too confining. Others want more touching, and climb onto their parent's laps so often that their parents yearn for signs of independence.

Parents may try to force hugs on an unwilling child, or force a clutching child to play with others. Parents should find other ways to show closeness, and encourage their child for their successes at independence.

We've all seen toddlers who are always clutching a teddy or soft blanket - that's normal. However, other children seem to be constantly stroking their teddies and blankets. These children are literally screaming at us that they're not receiving enough touching. They compensate for this by stroking their teddies and blankets.

If you've recognized this tendency in a child close to you - do your best to change the situation. Unfortunately, this is not as easy as you might think. Many parents (when they realize what their child has been telling them non-verbally) try to hold and cuddle the child. The child promptly pushes them away and reaches for and strokes their teddy or blanket (which has been their substitute for your touching). The parent feels rejected, and may quit trying.

Don't give up! These are the kind of children who could grow up with an invisible barricade around them. When they become adults, people might say about them, *"I can never get close to him or her. I've known him or her . . . years and I still don't know much about him or her."* These are terribly lonely people because they hold others away from them mentally, emotionally and physically.

"How can I get my daughter to accept my hugs?"

Use any reasonable means you can to have her accept touching. Accomplish this by sitting beside her while she watches television. While she's distracted, pull her onto your knee. She may not stay long the first time, but as her comfort zone increases, she'll allow longer and longer periods of cuddling. Have her sit on your knee so you can both crayon in a colouring book. Or she might enjoy receiving a back rub. Try this when she's settling down for the night.

Explain how other close family members can give more touching as well, but make sure they don't intimidate the child with too much touching too quickly. Don't forcibly remove children's teddies or blankets! Let them bring their pacifiers with them. Soon the child will leave his or her pacifiers behind.

Self-touching

"My son Danny has suddenly started holding his genitals and sometimes masturbating in public. How can I stop this without making him feel as if he's committed a sin?"

All children are curious about their bodies, and soon learn what feels good and what doesn't. He's learned that he likes to hold his genitals. Do ensure that he doesn't have a rash or some other physical reason for his behaviour.

If you've been able to rule out a physical reason, explain to him that it's not good manners to touch, rub or scratch himself in certain areas of his body (show him where) when he's in public. Explain that those type of actions should be conducted in private (similar to when he uses the toilet - it's a private thing).

124

The Canadian Mental Health Association were kind enough to give their permission to include the following information in this publication:

"Why won't she listen to me?"

A close look at development and discipline

One mother asked, "How can I get Jane to do what she's told?" Of course total obedience isn't the answer. The goal is not to control the child, but for the child to learn self-control.

Here are some ideas that work for others:

125

Some disobedience is a healthy sign. It comes with a child's curiosity, enthusiasm, new skills, new friends, changing emotions.

But that's not to say disobedience should be ignored.

As part of the family, your child has to learn the rules of the game. He has to understand other people's expectations and limits. He has to get along in cooperation with family and friends.

Much of this self-control is learned from other children. Some is learned at home. No one can tell you precisely how to encourage your child's self-control, but there are some basic principles.

Guides to self-control

1. A child's healthy development depends upon your obvious love. This should be at the heart of all family relationships.

Your child needs encouragement to develop self-control. As mentioned often in this series, sharing time and activities with a youngster helps to build a solid foundation of affection and trust. Time for story-telling, a game of cards, even setting the table.

When you must correct or criticize, talk about what he did. Say *"That was a bad thing to do."* Not *"You're a bad boy."*

2. A child's boundaries change year to year. Every child tugs and pulls to find out just what his limits are. In early years he may fight bedtime or limits on play. Later it's homework. Once he's a teenager, he's particularly anxious to run his own life.

Be friendly and fair. Trust him within the limits you set. He'll moan and complain, and although he won't show it, he'll appreciate that you care enough to make rules.

3. Firmness with kindness is the best approach. Yelling and shouting bring only more yelling and shouting. If you *expect* cooperation, you're more likely to get it.

4. Set a good example. If your attitudes and behaviour show little self-discipline, you can't expect much better from your child.

If your clothes are all over the floor, why should his be in the closet?

126

Routines and freedoms

By the time your child starts school, he should
have a daily timetable of what's expected of him:
breakfast time; lunch time; school time; dinner time;
bed time; daily routines of washing; brushing teeth;
making the bed; taking out the garbage.

It helps to pin this schedule on a wall near his bed
or on a kitchen notice board.

Give him some freedom to choose his own
friends, movies, records, clothes, ways of spending
his own money. He may make mistakes but he will
learn from them.

Avoid battles by planning ahead. Children have
little understanding of time. When you call, *"Lights
out in ten minutes,"* you give him a chance to see the
end of his television program or finish a chapter in his
book.

Disobedience and flare-ups sometimes grow out
of boredom, loneliness or fatigue. If your family
works together to understand and enjoy each other,
you'll be better able to handle emotional upsets.

Be firm — but on his side

Avoid nagging. Your child only learns to tune out.

Bribes seldom work. In fact, your child may soon
be a shrewder bargainer than you.

Threats are ineffective; the youngster may call
your bluff.

Avoid harsh spankings; they only lead to
resentment and more disobedience.

Be realistic and make sure the child knows you
are on his side.

What to do
when you blow your top

We all lose our tempers now and then. If it
happens rarely and you deal with it at the time, the
incident can be quickly forgotten.

Talk openly about your feelings and why you are
angry.

Try to explain how you, as parents, have learned
self-control: a walk to blow off steam when you're
angry; doing unpleasant chores first so you have more
time for hobbies...

Two important words:
love and limits

Self-control is an important quality for every child.
But the learning process can be exhausting.

When the going gets rough, remember this: *love
him and limit him.* His boundaries are gradually
relaxed to give him more and more freedom of choice,
but at all times there's plenty of family love.

It's a pretty good way to develop a healthy
personality.

CHAPTER 9
PROBLEMS WITH CHILDREN

Parents face many troublesome issues as their children grow up. Here are some of them:

Nervous Habits

"My wife and I are expecting our first child. When I see children sucking their thumbs or biting their nails, I see red and feel like stepping in to stop the habit. Other parents appear oblivious to this behaviour. How can I keep my children from starting these terrible habits in the first place?"

To many parents, these nervous habits signify that there's something emotionally wrong with the child. In reality, twenty-five per cent of all children, develop nervous habits that comfort and soothe them when they face difficult situations. Concentrate on finding something that's comforting for the child that won't develop into a full-blown negative habit later.

Negative habits include, nail biting, thumb or finger sucking, sucking or picking at clothes, twirling or pulling their hair, plucking their eyebrows, blinking of eyes, clearing their throats, shrugging their shoulders, cracking their knuckles or tapping their feet. Others make repetitive movements such as rocking (baby rocking itself to sleep in its crib). Most habits disappear in three to twelve months. When children are under increased stress, many fall back into their habitual behaviour even when they're four or five years old.

Parents should never punish a child for a habit. Instead they should look at what's happening to cause the child stress, and work on relieving that stress in a more positive way.

My personal answer to thumb sucking is that many children do not have their sucking impulses relieved, so find the first item they can to put into their mouths. This is often a finger or thumb, but others suck on blankets and sleepers. By providing a safe, well-designed pacifier, the child will relieve their sucking instinct and can throw their soother away themselves when they no longer require it.

My children all used pacifiers but none seemed to suck fingers, thumbs and blankets. One child was a rocker, and we'd often have to force the bedroom door open when he rocked his crib across the room blocking the door. Placing rubber stoppers under the wheels and moving it away from the wall allowed him to rock peacefully (usually five to ten minutes) without disturbing others.

Late Pregnancy

"I just learned that I'm pregnant at 39. My two other children are ten and fourteen. What positive or negative effects will this likely have on my existing children, and what kind of problems could my 'late arrival' cause?"

The negative effect to you personally, might be that you feel this will stop you in your tracks career-wise. You also might wonder whether you will have the energy necessary for another eighteen years of parental responsibility. You may feel isolated when you look at your friends, with grown children, and wonder if this will affect your social life. Your children might object to the situation because none of their friends' mothers are having more children. Or strangers might embarrass you when they assume that your newest child is your grandchild.

Late pregnancy has many positives as well. You may have reached many of your career goals and welcome the diversity. Your older children will gain valuable experience in caring for an infant and later a young child. You'll have built-in babysitters, because your existing children are old enough to give you substantial help.

Many new parents unfortunately have not had this opportunity while they were growing up. You've gained valuable experience from your older children, so will probably feel more confident in your ability to raise a child.

Terrible Twos

"Child-raising experts have said that I should make every effort to say 'No' as seldom as possible to my children, and that I should stop and explain why I need to say 'No.' How can I do that with my two-year old who is constantly in motion, into everything possible, and happiest when I turn my back and he can discover yet another new way to get into trouble?"

It really isn't practical to say, *"Jenny, it would be better if you didn't put your finger into that electrical outlet. If you do, you'll find yourself with permanently curled hair."* Or, *"I'd rather you didn't dunk your toys in the toilet because it's unsanitary."* Or, *"Please don't eat that dead fly. I have something much more appetizing for you."*

When the children are in danger, a sharp *"No"* may be the only suitable reaction (no matter what their age). In non-emergency situations, instead of using the *"No"* word, distract the child with activities they CAN do. If children are too young to reason with, this may be the only solution. As they mature, add reasoning to why they can't do something.

Hyperactive child

"My son is so hyperactive that I have trouble settling him down at night."

He needs a calming down period before bedtime. If he's having trouble settling down for the night, try the following:
* Make sure he's had his bedtime snack and has visited the bathroom.
* Have him lie down on his bed.
* Ask him to relax and close his eyes (no peeking).
* Give him a gentle body rub, from his head to his feet (watch you don't tickle).
* Then, with feather-light touch stroke his forehead, cheeks, and chin with your fingertips.

By the time you're at the last stage he'll usually be dozy and comfortable. This works well for over-tired children as well.

Decisions, Decisions

"Marian is four years old. She takes forever getting dressed in the morning, and she ends up with clothes all over her room before she decides what to wear. This often results in me yelling at her and almost being late for work. How can I get her going in the morning?"

The first step is to eliminate the choices she has to make in the morning. The night before, put two choices of clothing out for her to choose from in the morning. In the morning, leave her with the two outfits, giving her a reasonable amount of time to get dressed. Show her on a clock when you expect her to be ready. Don't allow for any arguments. If she isn't ready on time (wearing one of the two outfits), help her get dressed and follow-through with a consequence by removing a privilege. Decide what privilege you'll remove from her (possibly no television when she gets home from daycare).

Tantrums

"My son is four and still has temper tantrums. Some little disappointment happens, and he's stamping his foot and screaming."

Though children lose their temper, and express their anger in inappropriate ways, it's important to look beyond the outburst to detect what caused it. You'll notice that behind every outburst is some negative feeling the child has not learned to cope with.

For instance if you told him to go to bed, and he resorted to a tantrum, you might find he was in the middle of an important game with his older brother (he was winning). This doesn't mean you give in to the tantrum. Instead explain that if he had told you about the importance of the game instead of screaming at you, you might have allowed him to finish the game. Point out that everyone has to deal with occasional embarrassing or frustrating situations.

Because he had a tantrum instead of explaining his need to finish the game, he'll have to go to bed without a bedtime story (or another withdrawal of privileges). Never reward unacceptable behaviour with privileges.

132

Try to get your children to solve their own problems unless they've become physically or emotionally aggressive toward with one another. If that happens, separate them and take steps to stop the behaviour from happening in the future. Look behind the behaviour to see why they're acting that way. Do they feel left out? Aggressive behaviour is often the way children express damaged feelings because they don't know any other way to express their frustration.

If he has tantrums in public, remove him immediately. Explain that in the future, he will have stay with a babysitter and miss special excursions because of his behaviour. This tactic is especially effective if there are other (better behaved) children who will accompany the parents while the errant child stays home with a babysitter.

Missing child

"I hate taking my two-year-old shopping because he insists on running around freely and refuses to sit in the shopping cart. I can't become distracted for a moment, or he's gone!"

Who's the boss here? Before you go shopping, ask the child whether he would prefer to stay with a babysitter or go shopping with you. If he says he wants to go shopping with you, he has two choices (a) he sits in the grocery cart or (b) you use a child restraint (usually a device that has a loop around the child's wrist that attaches to you in some manner). There will be no alternatives. If the child whines and cries, you will leave him at home the next time you go shopping.

"My biggest fear is that my child will go out to play, and simply disappear. How can I keep myself from panicking when-ever my child is out of my sight?"

You've just described a parent's worst nightmare. Headlines often shock parents into taking emergency measures. They forbid their children to visit parks on their own, walk them to and from school and warn them repeatedly about not talking or going with strangers. Unfortunately, overreacting parents can alarm children needlessly. What's the answer? It's street-proofing your children. They won't learn this by running at the sight of a stranger. They require tools to enable them to determine themselves when a situation isn't right.

133

When your children can play with playmates on their own, ensure that they understand that you must always know where they are. Having your children call you when they're leaving their playmates' homes will enable you to watch for them as they travel home. You might ask the other mothers to call you or walk them home.

When your children understand what to call body parts, ensure that they know their body is theirs alone and they have permission to refuse any touching that feels uncomfortable. They are to tell you immediately if this happens.

Ask your child such questions as, *"What would you do if a stranger offered to give you a puppy or ice cream cone if you would go with them?"* Explain that they should not accept gifts from people they don't know. On the other hand, make sure your child knows whom they could go to for help, police officers, block parents, and teachers. Discuss what they should do if you lose them in a store, or they wander away from home.

If you're still upset about this, contact the block parent organization in your area for specifics. There are many good books and videos available to help parents and children develop street-smarts and safety skills. Most are free in libraries and many video stores.

Videos include:
> *Kids Safe* (when to call 911, first aid, fire & safety, handling strangers)
> *Strong Kids, Safe Kids* (strangers, child abuse and abductions)
> *Kids Have Rights Too* (child abuse, privacy, carefree childhood)

Books include:
> *Benjamin Rabbit and the Stranger Danger,* by Irene Keller
> *Play it Safe*, by Kathy Kyte
> *Who is This Stranger and What Should I Do?* by Linda Girard
> *How to Raise a Street-smart Child*, by Grace Hechinger.

Favouritism

"The other day, my daughter stated, 'You love Jimmy better than me.' She was terribly upset when she said this, and I think she really believed that her comments were true. My wife and I bend over backwards to treat our children equally. What's happening here?"

Start by asking her why she feels that way. You could be showing favouritism to one child over another and not be aware of it. Analyze how you really feel about your two children. I have two handsome natural-born sons and a beautiful adopted daughter. A year after her adoption, a friend asked me the following question, *"If your home was on fire, and you could save only one child, which one would you save?"* My answer was swift and sure, *"I'd help the most helpless one."* which in this case, would have been my adopted daughter who was five years younger than her brothers. My sons knew what to do in case there was a fire, so the likelihood of them saving themselves was certainly much better than a helpless infant.

It's common and normal for people to prefer one child over another, but they must work towards being less biased. Question your responses to your children's behaviour, to see if you're allowing favouritism. Do you expect similar behaviour from all your children, or do you let your favourite get away with actions you reprimand others for? Always keep in mind that it's the behaviour of the child you're objecting to - not the child itself.

It's especially difficult for parents when a child is noticeably different in temperament than them. The child may be outgoing and gregarious, whereas the parent is quiet and contemplative. Accept that you're different and go out of your way to adapt to their different personality types by encouraging their different talents and abilities.

For instance, you might say, *"I wish I had your knack of communicating with others. You can always say what you want to say, when you want to say it."* Everyone highly regards this type of compliment.

If you catch yourself showing favouritism, admit it to both yourself and your children and vow not to do it again.

Dealing with Bullies

"My eight-year-old son is anxious and unhappy. He complains of tummy aches with no medical cause. He resists going to school and his grades are dropping. Suddenly, he's having nightmares and cries at the slightest incident. He finally explained that a boy at school was pushing and shoving him, trying to make him fight and was making his life miserable. How can I help him deal with bullies?"

Bullies get a kick out of upsetting others and beating them up. Their victims are often quiet, suffer in silence and don't seek help. Bullies are visible, so usually get counselling, but their victims are the unseen problem.

Start by having a discussion with your son's teachers. Many elementary schools help these bullied children by offering special clinics for them. They act out "bully" parts where they're subjected to name-calling and teasing, so they can learn effective measures when dealing with aggressive playmates. Often the role-playing situations are from problems experienced by one of the group members.

The classes concentrate on building the self-esteem level of the child which helps them send the message that *"I'm not someone you can easily victimize."* It becomes easier for them to tell the other student to stop teasing them, or walk away from a threatening situation without feeling like a failure.

If the teacher is un-cooperative, speak to the principal. Another approach is to speak to the bully's parents. Unfortunately, children who are bullies often come from dysfunctional homes, and their parents may not cooperate and help solve this problem. One last resort, contemplate getting the police involved by lodging assault charges on the bully. Often having a police officer reprimand the bully will result in positive changes in the bully's behaviour. Do everything you can before resorting to changing schools for your child.

If parents observe their child displaying hurt or angry feelings, by wilful destruction or excessive anger towards others, it's possible they're bullies. They display this is by throwing things, breaking another's toys, or hitting or biting others. It's important to analyze what's behind the child's destructive behaviour. If this pattern of behaviour shows up in early life, professional help may be in order. If not dealt with before the child enters the school system, their destructive pattern may escalate until others (teachers) will insist that they get professional help.

When children's destruction of an item is deliberate, you can help them handle the results by stressing the rights of others. Then, identify the costs of repairing the broken item. The child should have to help to replace or fix whatever they broke. They can't replace it, unless they have enough money so you can identify tasks s/he can complete to pay for the damages. (This is one strong argument in favour of regular allowances for work performed).

Shy child

"My young son is such a shy, lonely child it's painful watching him. What can we do to help him?"
Children's shyness and loneliness can be a developmental phase or could be part of anxieties and vulnerabilities that could last a lifetime. We're all shy or feel lonely or anxious under certain circumstances. There are two basic kinds of loneliness:

* Social Loneliness: which comes from not having friends to play with.
* Emotional Loneliness: which happens when the child can't express his or her innermost thoughts.

Shy children often feel anxious. Anxiety includes a racing heart, sweaty palms, blushing or feelings of panic. Many are good at masking these feelings, but your son hasn't progressed to that stage. Younger children are more perceptive than we think. They pick up tension and turmoil in the home and often act out their feelings by being shy, clinging and anxious.

He could be uncomfortable around new people, new foods and new challenges. To most children, this is a passing phase. Don't allow others to tease the child about his shyness. Watch that you're not giving your child negative tapes by labelling him with derogatory labels.

Encourage your child to rehearse difficult situations with you, acknowledging that these situations can be hard to get through. Stay clear of placing your child in overwhelming situations, such as family gatherings where there are too many people for his comfort level. You might let him play in a room with a favourite cousin, rather than insist that he join the rest of the family.

Give him the opportunity of being the knowledgeable one, by inviting a younger, quiet youngster to visit. It's likely he'll be the leader that can be the self-esteem boost he needs. If he expects to be part of the "elite" group at school, point out that popularity is not always as fulfilling as friendship. Explain the benefits of having a few friends he really likes.

A good book on the topic is, *"Shyness: What it is, what to do about it."* by Dr. Philip Zimbardo.

Rejected child

"My son told me a story about what happened at school the other day. I was appalled by what he told me. Everyone in his class had received valentines from each other except one boy. At least half the class (mainly boys which included my son) had signed a home-made card that identified what a 'nerdy nut-case' the boy was. There were other more descriptive clauses as well. How should I have dealt with this situation?"

Start by asking your son, *"Why did you and your friends do that to the boy."* (It's possible that their action was a retaliation against something the boy had done to one of them earlier).

Then ask, *"What do you think would have been a better way to handle the situation? How would you feel if you'd received that card? What do you think you should do when you see the boy again?"*

Try to encourage your son to see the other boy's side of the issue. It's unfortunate, but five to ten per cent of elementary school-aged children receive rejection by their classmates at school. These children may be egotistical, bossy and obnoxious. Others receive rejection because of their restricted academic or physical ability or because of their physical unattractiveness. Some may not be accepted because of their withdrawal from others, their clothing style, religious or ethnic background or even a different first name. Children with aggressive attitudes promote the most noticeable rejection from other children. Often these children's only friends are other aggressive rejectees.

Not only do these children have unhappy childhoods with few if any friends, but they're prone to a myriad of problems later in life such as depression, truancy, or problems with the law. Rejected teens drop out of high school seven times more than accepted students. Mental health problems in adults often evolve around whether others accept them during childhood.

"My son was the one who received the valentine's card!"
Examine your child's behaviour to see if any of these apply to him. Is this an isolated incident? Concern is necessary only if he's repeatedly rejected over a long time. Does he have close special friends, ones that others don't reject? When you observe him with others, what behaviours could he be using that need adjustment? He may need help with his social and problem-solving skills. Popular children feel in control, and it's possible that your son doesn't feel in control.

He probably needs self-esteem boosting that would come from authentic compliments from the adults in his life. When he feels good about himself he won't feel the need to "act out" his frustrations by either aggressive behaviour or withdrawal. He'll feel more in control of his life. Your goal should be to ensure he's comfortable with himself and confident in his behaviour. If your efforts in this area don't work, consider professional counselling.

Change in behaviour

"My seven-year-old son has changed behaviour drastically in the past month. He's gone from a well adjusted happy boy to one who's behaviour swings between throwing tantrums and withdrawal. How can we investigate this matter without making matters worse?"
Start by talking to him. Talk about the behaviour he's showing and ask him (in a non-threatening way) what's happening. *"It's not like you to have tantrums and get angry this way. What happened to make you so angry?"*
Do the same for his symptoms of withdrawal. You might find that he's facing serious problems either at school or with his peer group. These behaviours are often the sign that someone at school is bullying the child. The suppressed anxiety and anger at their predicament come out as tantrums at home. This is

where he feels safer in expressing his anxiety, frustration and anger. Knowing you care about him will start you both on the way to solving his problem.

If he clams up, talk to his teacher, and even his friends about his behaviour so you'll know what hidden problems exist for your son. Don't let the situation slide or his behaviour is likely to worsen. Consider getting professional counselling if the above attempts do not correct the behaviour.

Manipulative child

"Our child has become an expert at manipulating us, his parents. In the past month he's begun the game of asking one of us if he can do something. If the first parent says 'No' he goes to the other (who has several times said 'Yes'). Because my wife and I come from different backgrounds, we often don't have the same reaction to requests. How can we deal with this child's manipulation?"

What's called for here is a united front from both parents. Establish house rules that deal with anticipated problems. For example, when is bedtime and under what circumstances can you vary its timing. Try to be consistent in your responses.

Watch that one of you doesn't become the "heavy" by using expressions such as, *"Just wait till your father gets home."* Give discipline *when* the action occurs. The only time you should put off discipline is if you feel you're not in control of your responses. Wait until you've had time to calm down before you tackle the issue.

When the child asks you whether he can do something, immediately ask, *"What did your Mother/Father say?"* You'll soon let him know he can't get away with his divide and conquer scheme any more. If you're not sure what your spouse would answer to his request, tell him you'll let him know. If it's something that he has to know immediately, state, *"Let's ask Mom/Dad what s/he thinks you should do."*

Tattling

"What do I do when my children tattle on others?"

The most common targets of tattling are brothers and sisters because tattling is part of rivalry. It's a method children use to ally themselves with their parents. They expect appreciation, rewards, extra love and attention. Tattling is a kind of power play. It's a way children attempt to make others look bad.

Toddlers may sound as if they're becoming tattle-tales but they may just be giving their parents information they think they should have. At this stage there's seldom malice intended by their tattling.

Consider the following:

1. Explain to the child that they're tattling and how you feel about this. The child must understand the difference between tattling about unimportant matters, and describing important facts, such as another child needing help. Your child must know they can come to you if they're really frightened about something another child is doing. This could be running into the street without looking to see if cars are coming or others are playing with matches.
2. Try not to pay attention to tattling, but don't ignore the child.
3. Don't assume that the tattler is right, and punish the person they tattled on. Investigate the situation carefully before acting, otherwise the tattler will believe you've condoned their actions.

Lying

"How can I tell when my children are lying to me?"

Let's face it, your children will have lied to you in the past and are likely to do so in the future. The usual reasoning behind lying is avoidance of punishment for a wrongdoing and later because of peer pressure. The older the child gets, the more convincing liars they become and the more likely they are to think that lying is okay. By the age of twelve, they no longer consider lying as always being wrong, and as adolescents, most become good liars.

Respect for parents helps children resist peer pressure somewhat, but peer influence increases with age. It's hard to fight the pressure exerted if your child gets in with a bad crowd. If necessary, parents may have to change the child's school or send him or her away for a summer with relatives.

Lying peaks at age fourteen, when they become more secure. Parents deal with them as independent people, the power struggle lessens, and they learn the high cost of getting caught. The smarter the child, the less they cheat, possibly because they realize that the consequences of getting caught, might not be worth taking the chance.

What parents do about lying, determines whether their children lie often and seriously. Younger children can learn from moral tales about people who lie. For instance (if they're sports buffs) explain that because Ben Johnson was charged with taking steroids, his lies keep people from trusting him now. Describe how the more they lie, the fewer people will trust them and the more they'll question their honesty. Identify the differences between little lies that save people's feelings, and lies that betray trust.

How can you tell if your children are lying? Watch their body language. When children are proud of what they've accomplished, they're open with their body language. They show their hands openly. When they feel guilty or suspicious, they hide their hands either in their pockets or behind their back. If you accuse them of something, they'll likely give you an incredulous look and reply, *"Who me?"* To try to make you believe them more they'll usually put their hand on their chest (a non-verbal sign of honesty).

Don't get in the habit of assuming your children are lying, it's better to be misled than disbelieve them when they're telling the truth.

When you do catch a child telling a lie, give separate discipline for the lie and the offence, making sure the punishment suits the crime. Explain that it's their lying you don't like, not them (deal with their behaviour not them as people). Look into why the child is lying. Could there be an underlying cause?

Show them by example by admitting your mistakes, then show how you deal with and correct your mistakes. See Chapter 4 - Body Language for more information on this topic. A good book on this topic is *"Why Kids Lie."* by Paul Ekman.

Phoney Illnesses

"What do I do when my son pretends to be sick?"

Look carefully at the times you believe your child is faking illness. Is it early in the morning and possibly he doesn't want to go to school? Is it only on rainy days. (Could he be afraid of lightening or thunder?) Is it when he has a test coming up?

Does it happen on the two days a week you work away from the home? (They want you to stay home, so you'll be there when they come home from school?) Watch that you don't instil feelings of panic in him by your actions.

Does your child pretend to be sick just before it's time for his piano lesson? Or does it happen in the middle of the night (which could be legitimate illness or could be that he's afraid of the dark)?

Children who complain regularly of illness might be unconsciously using their bodies to express unhappiness at what's happening in their life or as a way of showing stress. It's a way of drawing attention to their problems that many parents overlook. They may copy symptoms they've seen their friends or other family members use to gain attention.

If your doctor has ruled out physical reasons and the child still complains of illness, rather than telling him that you know he's faking sickness, reassure him that you want to find out what's causing his illness. Talk about the feelings he's experiencing when he complains of pains. Ask about school work, how he's getting along with his friends, and anything else you think could be causing the difficulty. This may release the child to talk about his hidden problems.

When he's healthy, give him extra attention, and show you value his company by spending time with him. If the illness persists and the doctor has ruled out physical illness, it might help to have the child (and often family members) by seeing a counsellor.

On the other hand, some mothers miss their children far more than the children miss them and suffer more separation anxiety. When they're accustomed to being the centre of their child's world, it can become lonely for parents to be on the fringe of their children's lives.

Some children miss school because of complaints such as headaches and stomach upsets. What frightens many of them isn't school, but leaving their mothers, who depend on their children for companionship and comfort. These parents may urge their child to go to school, but their non-verbal behaviour shows that they're still wanted at home. They worry constantly about the youngsters' health and keep them at home for the least sniffle. Often professional counselling is necessary to break the cycle. To ensure this doesn't happen, parents must have other interests besides their children. This is where good friends, hobbies, and challenging lifestyle are the best defence against the loneliness.

Sex stereotyping

"My wife and I were stunned when our five-year-old son said to his infant sister, 'Too bad you're a girl. Boys are better. ' Where does that come from? What did we do wrong?"
Children go through many stages in finding out what they are and who they are and how they fit into society. Regardless of why it happens, by age two or three, children know they're girls or boys and have a sense of where they and others fit. Between six and eight, the usual boy no longer wants anything to do with girls and vice versa. A question we could ask is; Does a young boy like to roughhouse because that's how his father plays with him, or does he like it because he is genetically predisposed to do so?
Children decide the sex of others by their outward appearances, their clothes, physical appearance, and hair length. A three-year old observing a man with long hair might insist that he's a woman and no amount of discussion will change this. A two-year-old can be quite upset if someone refers to them by the wrong sex.
Preschoolers often mix fantasy and reality. For instance, they might believe that men are smarter because they have big heads; because their babysitter is a girl, all babysitters are girls; because their doctor is a man, all doctors must be men. Parents would counteract these comments by asking why the child thinks men are smarter and reminding the child about the time his mom figured out how to fix the toaster, that the teenaged boy next door babysits for the Smiths, and the doctor who operated on their dad last year, was a woman.
Later the child asks *"Who am I?"* and will imitate the same-sex parent and seek playmates of the same sex. By five or six it's *"Not only, am I a boy, but I'm a boy forever. Therefore, being a boy must be good - being a girl must be bad."* And by the fourth grade children dislike the opposite sex intensely. Now, there's powerful peer pressure for a boy or girl NOT to play with each other, even if they've been friends since they were toddlers.

144

Parents need to be positive, non-sexist role models. Consistency is the key. Watch your stereotypical remarks such as, *"That was typical of a woman/man to do that!"* Role models strongly influence children, and parents are the closest role models they observe. If you detect there is stereotyping at school, or find the system discriminates against boys or girls, please step in and address your concerns. Teachers should encourage the interaction of children by making sure that boys and girls share activities equally.

Food hassles

"My twelve-year-old son eats the darndest food. The other morning he left the house eating a piece of cold pizza and drinking a milkshake for breakfast! How can I get him to eat a decent breakfast without preaching to him?"

Not everyone likes cereal or toast for breakfast. Before you dismiss the credibility of your son's breakfast diet, you should be aware that children have some powerful allies for their unusual food preferences. The newest national nutritional program for children states there's nothing wrong with either milkshakes (providing they're made with yogurt) or pizza for breakfast. They also approve of leftover spaghetti, chicken, chili or a baked potato if that's what the child wants for breakfast. When your child refuses to eat vegetables, offer fruit instead. If it's peanut butter sandwiches, serve with fruit and milk.

Giving children choices (ones that are acceptable to parents) allows children to assert their independence while increasing the likelihood of them eating what you've offered.

Many young children dislike foods that are salty (such as olives). Most will refuse anything with a bitter taste, and research suggests that their reaction to bitterness may be an instinctive reaction that protects them from eating something lethal. Other children will balk at all new foods until they become used to them.

"My daughter refuses to eat what I serve. Does this mean that I allow her to eat whatever she wants?"

Avoid offering too many choices to a finicky eater. Instead of asking what she wants for lunch, ask whether she prefers scrambled eggs or a ham sandwich. Let her know she

145

has to stick to those two choices. Don't force her to eat something she doesn't like or want because it will likely cause her to dislike the food even more. If she refuses what you offer for lunch, remove it and explain that she can't have anything until dinner. Make sure you follow-through.

Have bread, rolls or fruit available at each meal so there are choices that the child likes. Set limits, continue to offer a variety of food and don't be afraid to let the child go hungry if s/he doesn't eat what you've served. If children don't behave properly, have them go to their room. Don't let them take food with them, return for dessert or eat until the next meal or snack time.

Never use food as a reward or punishment because it can result in eating disorders.

Daydreaming

"My daughter's in a world of her own. She's forever daydreaming. The other day, she went upstairs to get her books, and I found her ten minutes later stretched out on her bed reading a comic book (oblivious that her school bus had left without her). Put her at the kitchen table with a colouring book and a bomb could go off and she wouldn't notice. What can I do to stop this?"

Most children daydream, while others become distracted easily. Being able to focus in on one activity at a time, can take years to develop. It appears that your daughter has mastered this skill and is hard to distract. The problem you're having is WHAT she's focusing on.

One way to help with daydreaming is to make use of it. It's a sign of your daughter's creativity. Encourage her creativity by having her write stories about what she's thinking about. Live theatre might appeal to her. Help her get her assignments and tasks completed, by teaching her how to make *To Do* lists. Inspire her to try to focus her energy on what she's doing instead of allowing her mind to drift.

When you ask her to do something for you, give her time deadlines, and encourage her to meet the deadline by stating, *"I'm counting on you to do this by four o'clock. Can I count on you to do it?"*

Sleep-overs

"Since she was eight, sleep-overs have been big events in my daughter's life. We've run into some difficult spin-off problems; she's often crabby the next day, and her younger brother and sister are often disturbed by the giggling and noise of having extra noisy, excited children in the home. I don't want to curtail her fun, but how can I deal with the disruption with the least amount of effort?"

Explain to your daughter and her guest(s), what kind of behaviour you will and will not allow. Determine consequences should the behaviour not be suitable (curtailing over-night visits?). Often two or four guests at a time can be just fine, but try to keep the overnight visitors down to a minimum number. Trial and error will tell. Stick to even numbers otherwise the group might exclude the extra child. Talk to your guest's parents to make sure they send their favourite blanket or toy, whether they're afraid of the dark or any other possibility that can disrupt their happy night.

Establish lights-out time and what hour you expect them to be quiet in the morning - then stick to it. Allow guests to call their parents to say good-night. Don't let the visit extend too far into the next day: your child and you may need the rest.

Twins

"My seven-year-old twin sons rebel terribly when I try to dress them alike. They look so cute, and attract a lot of attention. I would think they'd like that."

Twins, even identical twins, are individuals. Don't stifle them by dressing them alike and giving them rhyming names. It's cute at the beginning, but it can become a problem when people don't take time to individualize and simply call them "the twins." Discourage twin "language" (which only *they* can understand) as they mature. In extreme cases, it can interfere with normal language development.

Children need to have some items that belong only to them. Don't encourage them to do everything together, although parents should not insist on separations of any kind. If they want to be together and are doing well, separation can be traumatic. They'll separate when they're ready.

Encourage them to make independent decisions as they mature, and keep in mind that eventually, they'll be on their own. If they wish more independence, grandparents can help out by having one twin visit at a time, possibly spending a weekend with them.

They should have separate friends at an early age. This is especially important if one twin seems to be less independent than the other. Separating them at kindergarten can encourage independence, as does separate bedrooms. Encourage teachers to pay attention to each twin's individual capabilities. They shouldn't compare them to each other (nor any other two siblings).

Summer Vacation

"In two weeks, my family is leaving on a two-week vacation. It will be an eight-hour drive until we arrive at a cottage we've rented for the duration. If it's anything like last year, the children will start whining five minutes after they get in the car and will spend much of the time at the cabin stating, 'What can I do? ' How am I going to survive the holidays?"

As any parent will agree, driving is not the challenge, driving with children is! Close quarters (being within arms reach of a sibling) the confinement itself (lack of movement) and the boredom of having to sit and "do nothing" can add up to a horrifying experience for all involved. Add a pet to this scene and it's chaos. Many parents (passengers only) resort to taking tranquilizers, and wish they had the nerve to give some to their offspring as well.

So how can children survive after the many new games (bought specially for this trip) have run their course? Have the youngest and oldest pair up rather than having rivals sit together.

Try using what's happening outside the window by playing a game called auto bingo. This is where points are given to the first child who spots:

--a red car, a blue station wagon, a car with four people in it, one with three people.

--the first cow, horse, sheep

--barn, haystack, farmer

Make the list before leaving on the trip or compile it while in transit. Each child will have a list and will get extra points for special items such as spotting a police car, an ambulance, or fire truck. This activity never gets mundane because the scenery keeps changing.

Before leaving, involve the children in the planning of the trip. An older child could sit in front with the driver and help navigate. Chart rest and food stops as you go, and bring out new games as you reach certain points on the highway. Building toys can keep small hands busy as can hand-held video games. Magnetic doodle boards can make for hours of fun. Teenagers can listen to their favourite music singly through headphones and younger children listen to books on audio tape with their own headphones.

If you have a portable audio cassette, buy an inexpensive microphone and tape your children singing along with music from the car radio.

Pack soccer balls, baseball and gloves for active play at rest stops. Be aware of the need for youngsters to stop for a bathroom break within a half-hour to an hour after eating.

When you reach the cabin and your children ask, *"What can we do?"* brainstorm with them to see what alternatives they have. Weeks before leaving on your trip, start listing alternatives you can suggest and make sure you have the items necessary for projects. For younger children, empty egg boxes, pipe cleaners, pompons, bits of felt, glue, eyes, childproof scissors, and other innovative items can be used imaginatively to make any number of creatures.

Get other children in the area of your cabin involved. Have them dress up in old clothes and put on a play. Another pleaser is to tie a rope to a tree, with someone holding the other end. Have the children see how high they can jump as you raise the rope - giving prizes to all participants. Then, reverse the process and have them go under the rope doing the limbo (fun to do to music).

For older children, tie a rope to a tree (with knots every eight to 12 inches) and see who can climb the highest, the quickest. Have them wear gloves for this activity. Place an inexpensive double blow-up mattress (or old mattress that can be lugged out of the cabin) under the rope so they won't hurt themselves if they fall. Be creative - encourage your children to be creative, and vacations can be fun.

However, don't plan *everything* for them. Leave lots of "hanging around" time so they can make their own fun at their own pace, with their own friends.

There are usually three stages to summer vacation for children. Each stage has it's own unique qualities:

Stage 1:
When school is over and they need to wind down, but still need a structured environment. It's an ideal time to register them in camp so they can let off their excess energy. If this isn't possible, children may welcome the chance of participating in swimming, art or computer lessons.

Stage 2:
This is a quieter time, about the middle of their holidays. Families should plan their holiday time for this stage if possible. This time should not be over-scheduled, giving the children time to adjust to the slower timing. You'll have to think of projects for them to do, but you won't likely have to keep them amused, especially if there are other children around.

Stage 3:
This is the final week or two of summer holidays where getting ready for school is of primary interest. By this time they should be rested and ready to get back into the groove and daily schedule of the fall, so encourage a faster pace.

Separation

"Our son Ben will be going to camp this summer and school this fall. How can we prepare him for those separations from us?"

If there's time before he goes to camp, have him stay overnight at his grandparents place, another relative or good friend. Make sure he has plenty of familiar objects that he finds soothing - his favourite baseball cap, video, jacket or whatever gives him comfort. Let him know how he can reach you should he need to get in touch with you. Have him practice writing letters (even if he hasn't left home yet). Many children have never written letters, so need some "warm-up" for the real occasion when they're away from home.

Death of sibling

"My wife and I have just learned that our three-year-old son has leukaemia and is not likely to live for more than six months. How can we prepare our two other children (six and nine years of age) for this eventuality and help them through it all?"

Demands on parents are so great during a child's serious illnesses, that their other children might feel neglected. They may believe that their parents don't love them as much, so can feel jealous of the attention given to the dying child. This leads to guilt feelings that they have bad thoughts about their brother.

Another real fear is that they might catch whatever it is, and die too, so they're reluctant to be near the sick sibling.

This is when close friends, teachers and grandparents can step in to make sure the remaining children have their questions dealt with, and feel loved and cared for. Encourage teachers to report any negative behaviour, so you can step in and correct the problem before it escalates. Parents often make the mistake of isolating their children from the sick child, which makes them wonder 'what's going on that I don't know about.' Other parents smother their remaining children with attention and overprotection.

The signs that your child is in trouble often start with outbursts of temper at home or at school. Grades may start to slip, or the child may be truant. They're often smouldering cauldrons of anger, guilt and feelings of abandonment. They often wish their sibling would die so they can have more attention, then feel guilty because of these feelings.

When someone close to a child dies, for some reason the child may feel that *they* made it happen. They need reassurance that they had nothing to do with their sibling's death. Parents wishing further information on this topic should read Betty Jane Wylie's book *"Beginnings: A Book for Widows."*

CHAPTER 10
DIFFICULT TEENS & YOUNG ADULTS

Some teenagers breeze through their teen years with only minimal disruption to themselves and their parents. But others, because they have so much trouble understanding themselves, have trouble understanding their parents as well and do things intentionally to annoy them. Their negative behaviour includes lying, defying authority figures, leaving their belongings lying around, and playing truant from school.

Trust

Parents need to start gaining their children's trust early. Children need their parents' trust to feel loved, but this trust can often break down during their teen years. Teens (who so far, couldn't wait to tell their parents everything), may suddenly clam up. This causes their parents to start imagining the worst: they're on drugs, they were drinking at a party, or having sex with their partners. Often the more invasive the parents' questions become, the less the teens reveal.

Don't pry, let your teenager have their privacy except in issues that are important. Make sure they understand the concept of "consequences of their actions." For instance, *"I don't want to force you to study, but I feel it's important to me as a parent to limit the time you spend watching TV until your grades improve."*

Parents should explain why they need the information they ask for and share their disappointment when their teenagers

153

break their trust. Give them a second chance. When teens feel their parents are trusting (not controlling) they'll volunteer information themselves.

If you haven't considered the following questions, think about them now, get your spouse's opinion, and see how you'd want to deal with the following situations:

1. What would you say to your daughter or son if you didn't approve of their choice of date?
2. How would you set dating rules (weeknights, weekends, curfew)?
3. Would you allow their girlfriend or boyfriend to study with them in his or her bedroom?
4. When do you think their sex education should begin? Would you do this by giving them books on the topic? How would you broach the topic, and what would you say to them? How far would you go in your explanations? At what age?
5. How and when would you talk to them about their own sexuality? With your daughter? Your son? Would you be as cautious and informative to both your daughters and your sons?
6. When would you discuss pre-marital sex, contraception and sexually transmitted diseases?
7. What would you do if your fifteen-year-old daughter came to you with the information that she was pregnant? What would you say? How would you feel about the father of her child? What would you advise her to do about her pregnancy or would you leave it up to her? Are you informed enough about the choices available to her? Would you support your daughter, no matter what choice she made?
8. How would this differ if it was your son who came home to say his girlfriend was pregnant. How would you feel about his girlfriend? What would you advise them to do?

If you have children entering their teen years, now is the time to consider these questions and come up with a plan of action satisfactory to both parents. This will prepare you for what you would do in these situations, and give some continuity to your actions should the need occur.

I'm glad I'm not a teenager right now. Drug and alcohol peddlers tempt them. They see members of their peer group smoking, drinking and taking drugs and many have been enticed into "just trying it," then find themselves hooked into an addictive habit.

At school, students are often inundated with nothing but negatives. They seldom hear from their parents and teachers about what they've done right at school, but they certainly hear about what they've done wrong.

Teens are far more upset by their parent's fighting than they let on. Some miss the opportunity of observing loving, nurturing parents who care deeply for each other. Without this daily exposure of how men and women can work together in harmony, they don't learn how to get along in romantic relationships of their own.

A large proportion of teens these days are living in broken homes and their parents have less time to spend with them. The absent parent often makes up for the time they don't spend with them by lavishing expensive gifts on them. When asked what they want from their parents, many teens would say, to spend more time with their respective parents.

Added to this, are the financial worries of a single-parent home. Teens fear they won't have enough money to do everything in life they hope to do. Often, an immediate need for money for education is a prime source of stress.

Others see both their parents working to keep up with the cost of living, and face the frustration of realizing that unless they have a good education, they too will be doomed to a low-paying job. They see universities and colleges entrance requirements raised higher and higher along with their costs. For many, no matter how hard they work, they can't see themselves being able to meet the minimum requirements. Parents should encourage them to do the best they can, and if necessary, get private tutoring.

Another focus of teenagers is their environment. They see the mess their parents, grandparents and ancestors have made of their universe, and have concerns about the quality of the water, air and food they eat, and how their world will be during their adulthood.

When a high school teacher wanted to find out her class's career aspirations, she asked, "What do you expect to be doing in five years?"

Her student's took her career-oriented question a different way than she anticipated. Over one-third of her class stated they didn't expect to be alive in five years - that they expected to die either in a nuclear explosion or because of pollution. Parents expected this four decade-old fear to be over when the Iron Curtain came down, but with all the uncertainty in the world and the third world countries having access to nuclear warheads, the problem still existed. What a legacy we've left our children!

Other problems her students identified were the poor economic situation and high unemployment. The students were aware that many university graduates were struggling to get a job and wondered if they should really care about the marks they were getting in high school. They felt it wasn't worth the effort to get good grades because there didn't seem to be many jobs available anyway.

At that time, the local unemployment rate was 10.5 per cent and climbing. There's no doubt there were many unemployed people, but they were concentrating on the unemployment rate. The "employment rate" should have been what they were watching. The employment rate was 89.5 per cent - still the majority of the population were working. The teacher explained that should they choose to let their marks drop, she could almost guarantee that they'd be in the 10.5 per cent group of unemployed workers. On the other hand, if they kept plugging along, they'd likely be in the 89.5 per cent who found employment.

Because most of them would be working many years of their adult life (male - forty-five years, female - thirty-five years) they have strong reasons for concentrating on finding the right job. Most will be employed in four (or more) occupations in their lifetime. Many surveys indicate that eighty to ninety per cent of employed people are in the wrong job. So choosing the right career is paramount. Once they've chosen a career - studying, learning, and achieving their ideal job should be where they concentrate their efforts.

Teamwork

One valuable skill teens learn through competitive team sports, is how to co-operate with their peers. This co-operation often stops at the end of the school grounds. Many teens come home, do little or nothing to help around the home, but have plenty of time to get into trouble.

In many homes, both parents or a single parent work full-time away from the home. Their children and teenagers often complain that their parents have no time for them. Their stressed out, hard pressed parents need to use the energy of their teens to help with the smooth running of their home. This way, the parents have more time for family activities. Parents initiate this by calling a family conference.

Family conferences

Whenever there's an important issue that involves the entire family, call a family conference. This could be when Mom goes back to work, when Dad gets a promotion and has to move to another city, when a relative is very ill and may die, or any other important family issue.

Family conferences are held to discuss problems within the family, to delegate new responsibilities and to touch base with how family members are doing in their lives.

To prepare for a family conference about delegation of tasks, a parent would write down all the chores that need completion around the home and yard (including *all* tasks). Copies of this list are made for each member of the family who's old enough to read. Then a family conference is called:

1. At the family conference, ask all members to volunteer for some of the chores. Then, the parents fill in the chores they feel comfortable handling.
2. The remaining tasks are then assigned. All members are free to negotiate and trade chores with an accepting member. Each person must know how and when they're expected to complete their duties.

3. Anyone trying a new task receives training.
4. One parent asks each family member, *"Can I count on you to do these chores competently and on time?"* Parents are to wait until they get a commitment is received from each member.
5. Parents also explain that they don't want to have to nag anyone to complete their chores properly.
6. Then, one parent follows-up, to make sure tasks are completed properly.

To make sure this process works, make sure you give rewards to your children - signs of love and appreciation. Acknowledge jobs well done, and arranged special family treats for exceptional work, for anything above and beyond the call of duty.

If you've received the excuse, *"I don't have time,"* help them plan their time. Try to avoid power struggles. If one teenager or child has the job of taking out the garbage, another has to clean the bathroom (including the toilet), another mows the lawn, etc. Start job rotation to guarantee completion of distasteful chores.

Touching older children and teens

We often forget that older children need touching too. This is especially true with pre-teen boys. They feel they're too old to sit on their parent's knee, and don't like relatives to kiss them. They appear to become untouchable, but still need touching. Roughhousing accomplishes this. This may or may not include parents.

A parent who does roughhouse, must remember that the child needs to win most of the time. Stay clear of situations where they feel helpless. Tickle only to amuse the child. Stop immediately if the child shows signs s/he's had enough. If tickling continues past this point, it becomes torture to the child, and is a form of child abuse.

A young teenager going through puberty, will signal they need more touching (sometimes after they've had a particularly stressful day) by asking their parents for touching. For instance, they might say, *"Mom, my back and shoulders ache. Will you massage them for me?"* Or, *"The calves of my legs hurt Dad, will you rub them for me?"*

And of course, when they become older teenagers, they're getting touching you wish they weren't getting! How are you going to handle their growing interest in sex? Don't leave this type of education exclusively up to the schools. Unless you've had an open relationship where your children feel free to discuss everything with you, they won't feel comfortable talking about sex either.

Sloppiness

One mother tried unsuccessfully to get her thirteen-year-old son to pick up his belongings when he came home from school. She always knew where he was by following the trail of clothes, books, shoes, and food wrappers. He retaliated and called her a "nag," and the battle was on. Because she worked all day, she wasted her valuable time either walking around the mess, or cleaning up after her son.

When she learned the skill of feedback, her approach changed to . . . *"Martin, I work hard every day, and I get very annoyed at your actions. To be specific, I'm tired of nagging you to pick up your belongings every day. I've reminded you Monday, Tuesday, and this is Wednesday . . . Can you tell me why you're still doing something that you know annoys me?"*

Martin growled, *"Get off my back Mom!"*

His mother replied, *"Well the situation can't remain the way it is. Because we all live in this house, we all have certain responsibilities. One of your responsibilities from now on, is to pick up after yourself. If not, I'll take some of your privileges away from you."*

"What privileges?"

"You need me to drive you to your hockey practices twice a week. I simply won't drive you any more."

"Okay, I get your point. If I pick up after myself, you'll still drive me to my hockey practices, right?"

"Right. I know I can count on you to do your part around here."

Martin started being more considerate, and his mother could stop nagging him. She realized she hadn't given him responsibilities suitable to his age group, and still pictured him as a younger child. She also realized that she'd had little, if any, time for herself due to the unnecessary work she had done for her son.

Out of Control Teens

As one father lamented, *"My sixteen-year-old son has been acting very aggressively lately. He shouts at his sister, his friends and is disrespectful of adults. He's also started throwing things when he's mad. He's right out of control. How can I deal with his disruptive behaviour?"*

Many community and counselling programs help troubled teens. If you find your teen is not responding to your efforts to help, call in professional reenforcement.

One community program that's been successful, pairs a model student with a teen in trouble. Trained counsellors monitor the teens' progress. The volunteer model student provides anything from help with homework, to companionship, to a shoulder to cry on.

Today it often seems that the children have all the rights. Tough Love groups advocate that parents have rights too. This organization has helped many parents who have incorrigible teens. It is a support group for parents. These groups are not there to blame anyone, because at this point, it doesn't matter what caused the problem. The issue is, how to solve the situation.

Find your nearest Tough Love group and get to a meeting. Parents can examine the following criteria to find out if they need the help of Tough Love. Assess your situation by checking any items in the following lists which describe your situation:

Your teenager has:
- Missed dinner
- Been late
- Been stoned or drunk
- Didn't come home at all

Your teenager has run away:
- Overnight
- For two days
- For a week
- For more than a week

Your teenager has been violent:
- Verbally
- Physically to the house or furniture
- Physically to you or your spouse
- Physically to other people
- In school
- With the police

At school, your teenager has been:
- Tardy
- Absent
- Playing hooky
- Suspended
- You've been called by the school for bad behaviour

At Home:
- You and your spouse argue about your teenager's behaviour.
- You have withdrawn from your spouse.
- Your spouse has withdrawn from you.
- You have not had a peaceful night's sleep.
- You hate to hear the phone ring when your teenager isn't home.
- You or your spouse have lost time from work because of your teenager.

Legally, your teenager has:
- Received summons
- Received fines
- Received tickets
- Been involved in accidents
- Been charged with drug incidents
- Been charged with drinking
- Been arrested

If you've checked two areas in the school category, two areas in the home category, and one area in the legal category, the crisis is building. If you've checked more areas, you're already in crisis and should contact your local Tough Love group for help. They can help when parents have tried everything else from the police to social services and find traditional methods don't work.

The key to the Tough Love approach is letting children be responsible for their own behaviour and the consequences of that behaviour. Parents need to set a "Bottom Line" - something they want to accomplish with their teenager. It might be something as simple as insisting they take out the garbage. Do it now, your family's future depends on it.

CHAPTER 11
PROBLEMS WITH TEENS & YOUNG ADULTS

As children grow and mature, becoming teens and young adults they pass through many difficult stages. On one hand they're treated like (and feel like) children, and on the other hand, they're treated like (and feel like) adults. Parents may face many crises as their children pass through these stages of maturity.

Here are some crisis parents may face:

PROBLEMS WITH TEENS

Aggressive Friends

"My daughter hangs out with a very aggressive group of friends. They're loud, obnoxious and cause problems to those around them. How can I help her deal with friends who have this aggressive side?"

    This aggression could be the result of:
1. Feelings of insecurity either at school or on the job.
2. Feelings of being underqualified in education, experience or knowledge.
3. Not recognizing their own skills, abilities, or achievements.
4. Under-using their skills and abilities.
5. Not fitting in with others (which could include racial or cultural differences).
6. Failing to feel settled into their lifestyle. They feel that something's missing, but can't determine what it is.

Those who believe they don't fit into their lifestyle (despite the reasons), are likely to act aggressively. Many aim their aggression towards their schools, their friends and their family. These negative attitudes can be turned around by:

1. Giving authentic compliments.
2. Explaining how valuable their efforts are to their family and friends.
4. Giving examples where they can do more than they're doing and showing confidence in their ability to succeed at trying new activities.
5. Recognizing when they try new activities, their accomplishments and be there should they not succeed.
6. Asking for their advice in areas where they excel. For instance: *"Could you help me balance my chequebook?"* if they excel in their accounting class.

Most of these aggressive people are very success oriented. Their drive for recognition could cause the person to set high goals for themselves so they can achieve further recognition.

Another asset is they often have a high energy level and are happiest when they're kept busy and occupied. Instead of their energy being spend in disturbing others, it could be channelled towards productive accomplishments.

Power stimulates these people. Give them some authority where they're in charge, when they can handle it. Compliment them on work well done. Aggressive people like to dominate the situation, and like to communicate in a straight-forward, often blunt manner. Frankness can be almost a fault with these people and they're reluctant to ask for help when needed.

You can see there are challenges when dealing with these people, but if you can re-channel their energies in the right direction, society as a whole will benefit.

Swearing, abusive language

"My daughter broke up with her boyfriend because he was abusive to her. He's been harassing her with nasty phone calls. One time I picked up the phone and he started cursing me and

threatened to come over and 'Fix me' if I didn't put her on the phone."

Abusive language, swearing or uttering threats are criminal offenses in many jurisdictions. Not only could the person have their telephone taken away, but they could be charged and prosecuted in court. Don't wait for the next phone call. Phone your local police department and telephone company to determine your rights.

Know-it-all

"My son John is fourteen and is consistently acting like a know-it-all. He argues with everyone and tries to change everyone's opinion to match his. I don't want to stifle his individuality, but I can't tolerate the attitude of superiority his actions represent."

Your son is likely in the full bloom of puberty where one minute he's a child, the other a young adult. He's testing his independence by defending his ideas. You're right in not wanting to hamper his attempts at independence, but he requires guidance so he won't become a pain in the neck to others.

Know-it-alls whether they're teens or adults should be treated as follows:

1. When they challenge your ideas, most are vague about why they believe what they do. Ask, *"Why do you think . . . ?"* Make them come up with facts to back up their beliefs.
2. Prepare for their challenging comments by knowing the facts about your side of the issue.
3. Use feedback if they persist, explaining how you feel when they're constantly challenging your ideas. Encourage them to use empathy by asking them how they would feel if others challenged everything they said.

Dating

"My daughter has just started dating, and I realize that I'm terrified to let her go out. I remember all the feelings I had when I was a young man, and KNOW that most of the young men are focusing on - sex, sex, and more sex. How can I let her go out knowing she has a good chance of being coerced or forced into going beyond where she wants to or should go sexually?"

Hopefully, at an early age you've established a communication line between yourself and your daughter. If the groundwork's in place, communication will continue, though there will be major changes in your child's need for privacy. Continue to empathize (major ingredient to communication) and put yourself in her place. Don't force on her, the values you had as a teenager. Life has changed, and parents must change with the times.

Most parents (fathers especially) are tempted to "grill" their daughter's dates to decide for themselves whether the young man is suitable and trustworthy. Nowadays, many daughters simply don't bring home their dates because of this fear, so it's important that you don't start on the wrong foot. Most young daters meet at a fast-food restaurant, then go wherever they decide to go, either as a couple, or as part of a group. This fact terrifies most parents, because they don't know where their daughters are, or with whom.

Parents of boys are mainly afraid that some young gal will coerce their son into sex, get pregnant and he'll have to marry her!

Encourage your daughter to invite her dates to your home for dinner and make (or buy) something they'd likely order themselves, such as pizza. Don't start grilling him. Instead, treat him as you would any of your adult friends. Discuss something of interest that happened to you at work, what's going on in the sports arena, or anything else that won't seem like a grill session. He'll likely open up on his own to answer your unspoken questions such as: where he and your daughter met, what school he goes to, what grade he's in, what he hopes to be when he graduates, etc.

The first meeting will decide for him whether he's comfortable being in your home. The more comfortable he is, the more open he will be about his background, morals and values.

Watch you don't set too many rules and regulations for her - this will just make her feel as if you don't trust HER. Do, however, quietly explain your concern for her safety, and what to watch for in relationships. When the opportunity arises, ask your teen questions about what she'd do if . . . . Identify what you feel could possibly be dangerous situations she may face. For example: Being out with a date, who's too drunk to drive (or

166

too drunk herself); her date's getting too friendly and she wants a ride home, or any other potentially dangerous situation.

Make sure she knows you won't lecture her - that you're there to help her out of difficult situations should they occur. Make sure she knows you're there when she needs you. Be prepared to extend the normal curfew under special situations.

When my daughter was growing up, I made an effort to know where she was going. She balked at telling me because she often didn't know herself. She couldn't understand why I left precise information about where I would be, especially when I was out of town. Then a family emergency required her to contact me immediately.

She related afterward, that she doesn't know what she would have done if she hadn't been able to contact me right away. Then she realized that I wasn't controlling where she went, but simply wanted to know where she was in case of an emergency so I could reach her. After that time, she changed her attitude and made sure I knew where she was or touched base wherever she was.

Boy Crazy

"What's happening to my daughter?   She's only twelve, but spends most of her time mooning about boys? Isn't she too young to be concentrating her efforts on that?"
That girls are boy crazy, is hardly news. But today's girls are going to extremes to get their man. Today's little girls are frequently starved for male affection (absent fathers). Peer pressure and the image of romance permeate life for these budding women. Their hormones are out of whack; one minute they feel very grown up and the next they feel like helpless little girls. Society shows them that being grown up includes having a boyfriend. Boys their age, aren't interested in girls. Their hormones have not begun to rage (wait a few years!)

Let her have her romantic ideas, but watch that she doesn't loose touch with reality. Empathize with her and talk to her about how her life is changing. Let her feel the excitement of what's in store for her, but also help her keep both feet on the ground when she shirks her daily responsibilities at school and home.

Think's he's in love

"My sixteen-year-old son has only known his girlfriend for two months and he insists he's in love. What are the real telltale signs that it's true love and not infatuation or simply sexual attraction?"

There are many signs that point to true love. Here are some of them - have him decide what he would answer:

1. When I consider whom I'd prefer be with - it's with him (her).
2. I find I've quit examining and sizing up other men (women) as potential mates.
3. I'm quite content with him or her as s/he is. I wouldn't change any of his or her major characteristics.
4. We respect each other's talents and abilities.
5. S/he doesn't try to change how I am or things I believe in.
6. I find him or her to be a very interesting person.
7. We respect and trust each other.
8. We feel we could be best friends for life.
9. This is the strongest relationship in my life.
10. We miss each other when we're not together.
11. We always think of each other - s/he's always present with me wherever I go, if only in spirit.
12. We feel excitement when we're with each other.
13. We have a special feeling about each other that we don't feel with anyone else.
14. We don't have to talk to be companionable.
15. We both want to surprise each other with little things we know will please each other.
16. We have a strong physical attraction, love touching, and ache for each other when we're apart.
17. When we're together, we're the happiest we can remember.
18. We love planning activities we can do together.
19. We're very protective of the other's well-being and are ready to defend each other.
20. We have a great deal of influence over each other.
21. We're on the same wave-length and often know what the other is thinking.
22. We would never deceive or be unfaithful to each other.
23. We like each other's friends.
24. We enjoy doing many of the same activities.

25. We feel we could grow old happily with each other.
26. We're capable of being very intimate - there are no barriers between us. We're freely able to tell each other how we feel and discuss situations that bother us.
27. I feel s/he had good role models. If s/he didn't, s/he's had counselling to make sure the cycle doesn't repeat itself.
28. We're not afraid to be vulnerable to each other. We trust each other not to hurt the other.
29. We're not together simply because we don't want to be alone.
30. We both want a partner, not because we need one, but because we want one.
31. We are fulfilled, and happy with ourselves as people.
32. We're there to help celebrate each other's good days and cheer and support each other through bad days.
33. We stand by the other when they're sick, depressed or vulnerable to others.
34. We encourage each other to have other lives with our families and friends.
35. We do not act possessively or jealous when we're in mixed company. Our trust for each other allows us to know the other will do the right thing.
36. We do not depend on each other to give each other a good day, we're able to do that for ourselves.

Sexually active teens

"My daughter came to me the other day and asked me if she could have birth control pills. I told her I had to think about it, and would give her my decision next week. I don't know what to do. If I give her permission to get birth control pills, aren't I condoning and encouraging her to be promiscuous? On the other hand, if I don't approve and she has sex anyway, she may end up pregnant. What's the answer?"

There's no pat answer to this question. Teach both boys and girls that sex is an adult activity. It's for grown-ups - for people who have the morals to decide whether to have a family, the ability to support one, and the wisdom not to use their bodies for the sole purpose of gaining attention and affection from others.

Have a heart-to-heart talk with your daughter. Make sure you explain all the aspects of the situation, and that you hesitate to give her permission because it will look as if you're encouraging her to have sex. Point out all your concerns including your fear that she will be exposed to sexually transmitted diseases (prepare by getting pamphlets explaining what these are). Ask her why she feels she is ready for sex. Explain that if she has to sleep with a boy to keep him, he's not worth having.

If she still feels she wants the pills, give permission, but urge her to be cautious.

Sexually Transmitted Disease & Pregnancy

"I'm terrified that my son or daughter will be exposed to AIDS. How can I make them understand how much I fear this possibility?"

Parents of both male and female teens fear the possibility that their teen might be exposed to sexually transmitted diseases. Instead of lecturing or threatening (which can inflame youthful rebelliousness) be frank about your feelings. Rather than telling your teen that sex for teens is wrong, explain WHY it bothers you. Explain your desire that s/he will show sexuality with tenderness, commitment and responsibility - not confusion and fear. You might think your views will not be seriously, but most teens respect their parents' opinions more than they'll admit.

Find out how much they know about sexually transmitted diseases and birth control. Don't take the explanation, *"We covered this at school."* Make them be specific. *"Exactly what do you know about this topic?"* Or, *"AIDS scares the heck out of me. I want to be sure you know about it so you won't be at risk."*

If your teen brings up the topic, *"A girl at school had to drop out because she's pregnant."* This may be the opportunity for you to talk about birth control. *"I guess she didn't know how to use birth control and where to get it. Do you need any information on this topic?"*

170

Telephone manners

"As a mother of three teenaged boys, I don't mind if girls call my sons, but I do mind when they don't identify themselves, or phone after midnight. "
    I have to wonder why you insist that callers identify themselves before letting them talk to your sons? Most teens would object to this invasion of privacy. For the after-midnight calls, talk to your sons, explain the problem and set some guidelines.

Buck-passing

"My son is a buck-passer. He always finds someone else to blame for what he does. 'His grades are poor because he has a bad teacher.' Or, 'He's not on the football team because the coach doesn't like him.' How can I get him to admit to his failings and stop trying to pass them on to others?"
    Parents can instil a sense of responsibility in their children by teaching them the consequences of their actions. For instance: *"You say your grades are poor because you have a bad teacher. How can you say that, knowing that you've refused to do your homework? And how about the football team - they told you that if you didn't get your grades up, you couldn't even try out for the team. "*
    Could you be too harsh with your discipline? When parents use severe disciplinary action for mistakes, there can be other adverse effects, besides buck-passing. This can include lying, cheating, and hiding of mistakes.
    Occasionally, parents should set an example, by admitting (in the presence of their children) to making mistakes themselves. The admission of an occasional mistake by parents demonstrates to their children that passing-the-buck is simply not acceptable.

Respecting privacy

"My son accuses me of butting into his affairs - that he wants more privacy. I need to know what's going on in his life. How can I make him know that I respect his privacy, but need to have certain information to ensure his safety?"

Teenagers' obsession with privacy can make parents uneasy. Their closed bedroom doors, carefully guarded school possessions make many parents feel rejected and not trusted by their adolescents. The secrecy increases the fear that they're hiding something.

Parents should treat their adolescent daughters and sons as they would want to be treated. This means no snooping into their affairs, reading their personal mail or journals. Your trust in them breeds their trust in you. The only exception to this is if you seriously feel they're using drugs or have stolen property. They must know that their right to privacy doesn't include the right to involve their family in illegal activities.

Feels left out

"My son Derrick was very hurt the other day because he received taunts from two classmates who he thought were his friends. He does very well in school and they teased him about being 'Teacher's Pet.' How can he deal with this without alienating his friends?"

His father encouraged him to determine what was causing his friend's behaviour and asked him how he thought he could resolve the problem.

Derrick thought they were ashamed of him because of his good marks. His father suggested, *"Do you suppose they might be a little envious of the marks you get in school? If so, do you think they might want you to coach them a little to help them do better at their school work?"*

Because he and his friends share an interest in hockey, he suggested, *"Do you think that if I joined my friends' hockey team that we might have more in common?"*

Father and son worked through the problem and Derrick decided to try the two approaches to see if he could improve the situation. Instead of retaliating or dropping his friends, he tried empathy and co-operation, and it worked.

Laziness

"My children have a lazy streak in them, but then, so does my husband. They put off chores until I end up doing them myself."

Have a family conference, then do what supervisors do in the workplace - find their *hot button,* and push it. Some motivators are:

* money
* better working conditions
* the work itself
* competition/challenge
* recognition for good work

* status
* security (or lack of)
* extra benefits/privileges
* awards, and above all,

What will work for your family? As a last resort cut your children's allowances and pay a neighbour's child to do the chores they haven't completed. If you're a working mother, make sure your husband does his share by making sure he's aware of the breadwinner, child and home care split of responsibilities (discussed in Chapter 5).

It's possible that your children only hear about their mistakes. It's normal and necessary for everyone, to receive praise and recognition for work well done. It's the best motivator of all. Try it, and see if the situation doesn't change.

Be aware that it's not possible to motivate everyone - you just can't motivate some people. Start by explaining exactly what you expect of them (in writing if necessary). Then, give them many opportunities to improve their performance. If they refuse to conform, use the feedback steps including the consequences should they fail again (you choose what happens - discipline, withdrawal of privileges, etc.).

Low self-esteem

"My daughter mopes around the house, saying she's a failure at everything. She has few friends, refuses to try anything new, and is starting to fail at school. Her lethargic, negative, attitude is starting to rub off on the rest of the family. There's constant bickering at the dinner table."

"My son has gone through a tremendous growth-spurt and is about five inches taller than his classmates. He takes a ribbing, because his weight hasn't caught up and he's quite

gangly and under-nourished looking. How can we help him through this difficult time?"

"My daughter is fine dealing with her classmates, but becomes a shy, awkward, backward teen when she interacts with boys. Our baseball team will be going to another city on a chaperoned bus for a game. A girlfriend of one of the players invited her to accompany the team. She refuses to go, stating 'What would I say? I'll probably make a fool of my self. No I can't go.' How can I help her be more comfortable in situations with mixed groups?"

Teens no longer seek the approval of their parents and teachers, they seek the approval of their peer group. Surveys taken in junior and senior high schools reveal that teenagers' main focus in life is often their relationships with their friends. Most teenagers suffer from low self-esteem at least part of their teen years. To them, everyone is more popular, better looking, dress better, or smarter. They're too tall or short, early or late bloomers, have acne and other skin problems, or are too heavy, thin, or dumb. They wonder how they're going to turn out (a frightening prospect when their body is doing such unusual things to them).

Many peer at themselves in the mirror, trying to picture the finished product, and seldom come up with an answer unless they strongly resemble a parent. Because early bloomers look older, society often treats them as if they ARE older (when they're not ready for that role).

Many parents make the serious mistake of comparing siblings in a family that results in bad feelings for all concerned. Just because Jane is an "A" student, don't expect Roland to be. Since Roland is doing his best, that's all a parent can expect. Accept him as he is. Parents who aren't sports conscious, might completely miss the fact that Roland is the star basketball player for his team and make light of this accomplishment. No wonder Roland is mad at his family. The only ones who fully appreciate him are his basketball teammates and those who follow basketball at school.

As parents, we have to understand how important it is to help our children know they have the right to state their wants and needs. Children who have developed a strong sense of their own value by the time they attend preschool, will normally get along well with other children. Respect your children's strengths and abilities. Praise their successes. They'll probably try to deny their successes, because most teens are embarrassed by any fussing they receive from parents. Secretly, they're very pleased at the recognition.

Everyone has a special ability or two. Help your teens cultivate theirs and identify the areas where they're likely to succeed. For instance: *"Marge, you did so well at learning how to play the piano that I think you'd probably do well with an electronic keyboard. Would you like to try one to see how you like it?"* Or, *"Jim, you love basketball so much, have you considered contacting the YMCA to see if they're looking for basketball coaches for summer camp?"*

Loss of parent's job

"I'm a single parent, and I lost my job recently. My two teen-aged children are devastated because I've had to stop all the extras. My daughter is into jazz and we had to cancel her lessons. My son had planned to go to hockey school this summer. I had to tell him we simply couldn't afford it, and we had to cancel the summer vacation we planned. How do we all get through this tough time?"

This time teens can really shine if you let them. Call a family conference. Start by saying, *"As you know, I've lost my job. This means that we'll have to do without some extras we've had in the past. Here is a list of these."*

This will probably result in groans and arguments about why you can't cancel. At this stage ask, *"What do you think we can do so you can keep these extras?"* Make them part of the problem-solving process. Go into the meeting with several suggestions. You might have heard that a neighbour is looking for someone to care for her children after school, or you noticed that local pharmacy has an opening for help. Recommend these openings to your children and encourage them to apply. This way, they take responsibility for solving their own financial problems.

If there is an absentee father in the picture, consider asking him to help with your family's finances during the crunch.

Wants too much

"My son keeps after me to let him spend far too much money on his clothes. I can't understand the difference between buying a sweat shirt for ten dollars and one that costs sixty dollars (except the name on it). What's happening to teens these days that they have to be clones of each other? I simply can't afford sixty dollars for a sweat shirt."

There's a great deal of competition in the teen scene. If one person has designer sweats, so do all his friends. If her friends have a phone in their room, of course she wants one too. This is part of growing up.

Parents who understand this stage is coming, should decide what they will and will not pay for, before speaking with their children. This way, teens aren't likely to pit one parent against the other. Discourage them from nagging you. Do, however, listen carefully to what they say - so you're not missing important messages. Tell them what you're willing to do. If they wish to buy something more expensive, they'll have to earn the money themselves.

Answer their plea, *"Everybody else can do this . . ., has that . . ., is doing..."* with, *"We're talking about what you can do, what you can have, and what you're doing - not everybody else."* Then, tell them what you're willing to do or have them do. Set a good example by explaining the items YOU want, but can't afford. Let them know that you too, have pangs of envy about what you want, but have to be realistic on what you can and can't have.

Let your teen help with problem-solving. When you feel you can't afford that expensive sweat shirt, have him join you in brainstorming about how he might get the money to buy one. Having a garage sale worked for one family, and everyone ended up buying something they need out of the proceeds. Be creative - there are solutions.

Exams

"For about a month before his exams, I worry about my son. He required high marks to qualify for the university diploma of his choice, but he just blew a test because he was too tired to think straight. He's facing three exams next week, has a part-time job

and has lab and test reports to pass in. On top of this, his hockey team has done well and they're likely to go to another city this weekend for a tournament. He'll have to cram half-way through the night to catch up. How can his mother and I help him through these intense pressures?"

Around exam time, many young adults suffer from stomach pains, headaches, stiff joints and a general feeling of panic. These are the typical reactions of someone who's under so much stress that it becomes distress. Encourage your son to drop activities that he doesn't really need to do, especially around exam time. He may have to give up the fun of playing in his hockey tournament, although he may need this kind of diversification to blow off steam. He should drop his part-time job during exam time. Because of the lowered income, you might have to help him out financially.

It's possible that he needs a tutor, or someone else to study with, to lock in his studies. Encourage regular breaks in his studies by having him join the rest of the family for a snack and encouragement. The mental relaxation will revitalize him as much as the snack and encouragement will. Let him know you're there for him to help him in any way possible. Be available - don't give him the impression that you're too busy (the problem with many dual-income families). Many students won't "bother" their parents when they perceive they're too busy.

Double standard

"My daughter came to me the other day and embarrassed me with her comments. She said, 'Why does society still have a double standard? I'm a fifteen-year-old teen, and I have sexual urges too, and get turned on by my boyfriend. Why does society insist that I'm not supposed to have sexual feelings?' How should I deal with this?"

Many teens find themselves torn between remaining true to the values their parents have instilled in them, and gaining peer acceptance by going along with questionable activity. Keeping out of trouble, yet keeping friends, takes self-confidence and skill.

177

Society's values have not kept up with the reality of present-day life. For centuries, society has had a double standard for males and females. Girls, more than boys, receive mixed messages from modern society. On one hand they're told they shouldn't mess around, and on the other they're assaulted by advertising that gives a clear message that sex paves the road to happiness. The media inundates young women with images of young women as sexual playthings.

Encourage her not to get upset about others' beliefs and to recognize that it's natural for her to have sexual urges. However, this doesn't mean she has to act on those urges. Provide her with the information she needs to choose the route she will take. She alone should make the final choice.

PROBLEMS WITH YOUNG ADULTS

She's not ready for sex

The following conversation identifies a problem identified at my dealing with difficult people seminars. A mother was not only distressed, but very offended by a situation both she and her daughter faced when they were dating.

She identified the problem this way, *"A while ago, I noticed that my very attractive twenty-two year-old daughter Barbara, was dating only occasionally. Mainly, she went out with her best friend, Karen. They usually joined a mixed group, but seldom did either young woman go out alone on a date.*

I questioned Barbara about this, and she admitted she was reluctant to go out alone with men because of the problems she faced. She explained that part of her reluctance was because of the terror her friend Karen had towards dating. Twice, Karen had been the victim of date rape - when she was seventeen, and again two month's ago when she was twenty-three.

'How did this happen?' I asked. Karen had told Barbara that she'd liked the two men, and didn't want to lose them by making them mad at her for demanding that 'No' meant 'No.' She hoped that they'd listen to her when she rebuffed their advances. Unfortunately, both men pushed her further and further sexually until they refused to stop. Karen said she felt

dirty and soiled after they coerced her into having sex she didn't want. She hadn't pressed charges, and didn't see the men again.

My daughter Barbara, on the other hand, _had_ insisted several times that 'No' meant 'No,' and found that this ended most of her relationships with men. She decided that it just wasn't worth the hassles, so went out in groups instead."

The mother continued, "This phenomenon still amazes me. I'm a single mom, and have run into the same problem, but with men who should know better. You'd think that as men mature, and their raging hormones have dissipated, that they'd be less inclined to push a woman further than she wants to go. Too many men have the mistaken opinion that what feels good to them, must automatically feel good to women.

I've had to drop several of these 'octopi' because they simply didn't hear me when I asked them to stop touching me sexually. Some seemed to have an invisible cord that went from their mouths to their hands. Even a simple good-night kiss resulted in one or both hands automatically landing on my breasts or crotch.

Others started more serious advancement on the second or third date, and acted as if there was something wrong with ME, because I wouldn't get into bed with them. They didn't consider, that if I had sex with them on the third date that I'd probably do so with all the men I dated. How could they want me sexually (especially with the AIDs scare) if they'd even considered that?

If a man's hugging and cuddling progresses to intimate sexual touching before I have a chance to really know him, I retreat, rather than let him come closer. If they would only back off, they'd find that, like most people, I like to be held and cuddled and would probably want sex if not forced into it. The more they push, the more I run away."

These men have not learned the difference between sensual friendship and sexual lust. Sensual friendship occurs when a couple hold hands, hug, stroke the other person's hair and cuddle while watching television. Most people are starved for this type of touching. Unfortunately society encourages the myth that touching between couples is always a prelude to sexual intercourse.

Men who insist on sex before the woman is ready, are on a power trip and want their wishes to supersede those of their 'weaker' partner. These men often turn out to be wife and child beaters. You and your daughter will have to be patient. There are many fine men who do not fit this mould who are worth waiting for.

Daughter's wedding

When a marriage breaks up and children live away from one of their parents, they may face unique problems.

"My twenty-five year old daughter is getting married next year. Her father and I divorced when she was six, and she had little contact with him for many years. She wants him and his second wife to attend the ceremony, but doesn't want him to give her away. Instead, she wants her older brother to do this because he's been more of a father figure to her as she grew up, than her father. She's wondering whether she should approach her father for financial help with her wedding, and wants me to do this."

If you're comfortable talking to her father, call him up and ask him whether he'd be willing to help with the wedding expenses. Later, your daughter should explain to him how she feels about his attending the wedding and her decision about her brother giving her away. The latter conversation should be a few weeks after you've talked to him, so he won't think that his financial contribution had anything to do with her decision to have her brother give her away.

Can't keep a job

"My son can't keep a job. He's tried many kinds, but can't get one he really likes. What should I do to help him?"

People get into the wrong job because of many reasons:
1. They don't ask the right questions on the interview to establish potential problems.
2. They impulsively grab the first job that comes along that pays more.
3. They follow the advice of others, instead of listening to their own instincts.
4. Because Dad was an engineer, they become one.

5. They assume they can live with a lower salary than they're used to.

He needs to get career counselling to find out what kind of job would suit his wants, needs and abilities. They'll help him identify the transferable skills he already has that he can use in other lines of work. For instance: Scheduling abilities, supervisory experience, attention to detail, and manual dexterity. He may have to get additional education or training, but eventually he'll get a job that he enjoys.

PROBLEMS OF YOUNG ADULTS AND TEENS

Chauvinism

"Why do men call women 'girls?' ' I haven't been a girl since I was twelve. How would men react if women called them 'boys?' "

"My boyfriend's best friend is a few years' older than him. He treats all women, including me, as if we're second-class citizens and is always spouting off with jokes about 'dumb blonds. ' I'd love to zing him back one of these times, but don't know how."

Chauvinism is behaviour displayed by both men and women who believe that the world should be exclusively male dominated, and that men are superior to women. Chauvinism is one of the many serious problems women still face in the work place.

There are two types of chauvinism. Some aren't even aware that they could be identified as chauvinists. These are often older men, or men whose upbringing, customs or home situation, kept women in traditionally subservient positions. Many of these men call women, "Dear" - because they ARE dear to them. They protect women; feel it's their duty to be the decision-maker and protector. This type of chauvinistic man doesn't mean to harm women or know that what they say, may be offensive to them. Therefore, a much gentler response from women is necessary. Tell them how you feel, and give them the opportunity of changing their annoying behaviour.

181

The other kind of chauvinism is blatant (open and obvious). You KNOW this person is out to make women feel badly - to keep them in their "place." Here's a sample conversation:

He: *"Give women an inch, and they'll take a mile. Pretty soon we won't have any say in what's happening in the world."*
She: *"Well, with 52% of the population being women and only 48% men, what do you expect - the same paternalistic society we've suffered through for centuries?"*
He: *"You women are all too aggressive. You're not happy unless you're castrating men!"*
She: *"You really can't handle assertive women can you? You still think we should 'Yes, sir' your every command!"*

The woman resorted to defending her gender. She could have stopped his original sarcastic comments by sticking to facts, and deciding what the man was trying to tell her. If she had done this, the following conversation could have taken place:

He: *"Give women an inch, and they'll take a mile. Pretty soon we won't have any say in what's happening in the world."*
She: *"What's happening that you object to?"*
He: *"Women want too many extras in the work place."*
She: *"What are these extras?"*
He: *"Equal pay for one."*
She: *"Do you feel women should be paid less for the same work as men?"*
He: *"Not really. But how about day care, why is it necessary? Too many women work. They should be at home with their families."*
She: *"How many women do you think work because they have to?"*
He: *"Not many."*
She: *"Statistics prove that over three-quarters of working mothers HAVE to work because their families can't survive without both incomes. Over half these working women are the sole breadwinners for themselves and their children. The children require adequate day-care. Therefore, it's not a frill, but*

a necessity for most women. Do you feel women should be shouldering the full responsibility, or should the men be looking after their half of the day care expenses?"

You can see that the woman is combating the chauvinistic remarks with facts, not emotions and keeps the man on topic. As the conversation progressed, he used less and less sarcasm and they ended up in a discussion rather than a debate.

Some women, won't admit it, but they have chauvinistic attitudes of their own. For instance: Some won't accept orders from female supervisors. They feel (consciously or unconsciously that only men should be supervisors, and question the ability of their female supervisors.

Watch your language, especially when addressing women in the workplace. Job titles and descriptive labels are being changed to include both sexes. Here are samples of those that have already been changed:

Used to be:	Now Proper:
businessman	*business executive*
stewardess	*flight attendant*
chairman	*chairperson, chair, or moderator*
serviceman	*service representative*
delivery boy	*courier, messenger*
foreman	*supervisor*
salesman	*salesperson*
	sales representative
	sales clerk
spokesman	*spokesperson, representative*
tradesman	*technician, skilled worker*
workman	*worker*
career girl/woman	*doctor, lawyer, dentist*
manpower	*human resources*

We have to watch that we don't go to extremes with this. For instance: What other name could we give a manhole cover - a personhole cover?

Doesn't call after date

"My pet peeve is when fellows take my daughter out. According to her, they have a wonderful first date and he leaves her with the comment, 'I'll call you Wednesday so we can plan something for the weekend.' And he never calls again! Why do fellows do this?"

I've asked many men this question, and they explain that it's a standard comment after a date, whether they're going to call again or not. If they don't want to call, it lets them "off the hook" and eliminates any embarrassing moments.

This is very manipulative behaviour. How much better it would be, if they were open and direct with their dates. If they don't think they'll call or see the woman again, they should just end the evening by saying, *"Thanks for the nice evening. I had a good time."* Period. Not, *"I'll phone you on . . ."* Or, *"I'll get back to you during the week."* Or, *"Let's do this again."* if they don't mean it.

CONCLUSION
ARE YOU READY FOR YOUR
DIFFICULT SPOUSES AND CHILDREN?

You've been given the tools that can empower you to deal with irate, rude, impatient, emotional, upset, persistent, and aggressive family members. These crucial people skills allow you to deal with all types of difficult people and circumstances. Learn these skills, and you can't help but enhance your relationships with your spouse and children.

Your proficiency in people skills, will help you to control your moods and keep you cool when you're under fire. You'll start on the road to understanding why men and women have such an arduous time communicating with each other, and why they're likely to interpret situations differently. If you practice the techniques you'll be able to:

* master your mood swings by maintaining control when faced with negative situations
* raise your self-esteem level because you're in control of your emotions
* keep your cool under fire
* stop wasting your precious energy on negative emotions
* turn off hurt, guilty or defensive feelings
* stop feelings and actions aimed at revenge
* give and receive criticism with more confidence

* know how male and female communication styles differ
* use various communication skills such as paraphrasing, feedback, listening and speaking
* comprehend the importance of non-verbal communication
* deal with whiners, bellyachers and complainers
* deal with difficult spouses, children, teenagers and young adults

Learn the techniques and practice them daily. They <u>do</u> work! But like any new skill, you'll have to use them unfailingly until they become spontaneous and automatic. If you do, you can look forward to being able to control how you deal with, and react to others.

No longer will you allow others to decide what kind of day you have. Because you've gained this control, your self-esteem level will raise accordingly. The more self-assured you are, the less stress and apprehension you'll feel, which will give you more stamina and enthusiasm. Use these skills and brace yourself for the success that will inevitably follow.

For more help in dealing with difficult people and situations in the workplace, order:

* DIFFICULT PEOPLE - **How to Deal With Impossible Clients, Bosses and Employees** (Key Porter Books, Toronto).

Watch for planned future sequels entitled:

* DEALING WITH DIFFICULT RELATIVES AND IN-LAWS,

* DEALING WITH DIFFICULT FRIENDS AND NEIGHBOURS, and

* DEALING WITH DIFFICULT PROFESSIONAL AND TRADESPEOPLE.

BIBLIOGRAPHY

Aylesworth, Thomas G.   **UNDERSTANDING BODY TALK** F. Watts, 1979.

Berne, Eric   **GAMES PEOPLE PLAY,** N.Y.: Grove Prwess, 1964.

Bramson, Robert M.   **COPING WITH DIFFICULT PEOPLE,** Anchor Press/Doubleday, l981.

Carter, Jay   **NASTY PEOPLE,** Chicago: Contemporary Books, 1989.

Cava, Roberta   **DIFFICULT PEOPLE: How to Deal with Impossible Clients, Bosses and Employees,** Toronto: Key Porter Books, 1990.

Eckman, Paul   **WHY KIDS LIE,** Penguin Books, 1989.

Elgin, Suzette Haden   **THE LAST WORD ON THE GENTLE ART OF VERBAL SELF-DEFENSE,** Prentice Hall Press, 1987.

Farley, Lin   **SEXUAL SHAKEDOWN: THE SEXUAL HARASSMENT OF WOMEN ON THE JOB,** New York: McGraw Hill, 1978.

Fast, Julius	THE INCOMPATIBILITY OF MEN & WOMEN: & How to Overcome it, Lippincott, Philadelphia, 1971.
Fleming, Don	HOW TO STOP BATTLING WITH YOUR CHILD, Prentice Hall, 1989.
Fleming, Don	HOW TO STOP BATTLING WITH YOUR TEENAGER, Prentice Hall, 1989.
Girard, Linda	WHO IS THIS STRANGER AND WHAT SHOULD I DO? A. Whitman, 1985.
Gordon, Thomas	P.E.T.: PARENT EFFECTIVENESS TRAINING, N.Y.: New American Library, 1975.
Hall, Edward T. Hall	THE SILENT LANGUAGE, N. Y.: Anchor Books, 1981.
Hechinger, Grace	HOW TO RAISE A STREET-SMART CHILD, Facts on File Inc. 1984.
Jukes, Jill Rosenberg, Ruthan	I'VE BEEN FIRED TOO: Coping with your Husband's Job Loss, Toronto: Stoddart, 1991.
Keller, Irene	BENJAMIN RABBIT AND THE STRANGER DANGER, Children's Press, 1986.
Killinger, Barbara	WORKAHOLICS - The Respectable Addicts, Toronto: Key Porter Books, 1991.
Kyte, Kathy	PLAY IT SAFE, Knopf, 1983.
Potash, Dr Marlen S.	HIDDEN AGENDAS, Delacorte Press, 1990.

Rapoport, Judith	THE BOY WHO COULDN'T STOP WASHING, Dutton, 1989.
Smith, Manuel J.	WHEN I SAY NO, I FEEL GUILTY, Dial Press, 1975.
Tannen, Deborah	YOU JUST DON'T UNDERSTAND: Women & Men in Conversation, Morrow, 1990.
Ury, William	GETTING PAST NO: Negotiating with Difficult People, N.Y., Toronto: Bantam Books, 1991.
Woititz, Dr. Janet G.	THE INTIMACY STRUGGLE, Health Communications, 1993.
Wylie, Betty Jane	BEGINNINGS: A BOOK FOR WIDOWS, McClellan & Stewart, 1977.
Zimbardo, Philip	SHYNESS: What it is, What to do about it, Addison Wesley, 1977.

The following seminars are presented internationally
by ROBERTA CAVA of
CAVA MANAGEMENT CONSULTING SERVICES
#1201 - 12319 Jasper Avenue,
Edmonton, Alberta T5N 4A7

Audio tapes available **Video Tape Available*

* *

PERSONAL DEVELOPMENT

- DEALING WITH DIFFICULT PEOPLE, 1 - 3 hours,
    1 & 2 days (2 books available) * * *
    NOTE: Our most popular seminar

- Create a Positive Image, 75 min., 3 hours, 1 & 2 days*
- How to become a High Flyer, 3 hours, 1 day
- Take Command of Your Future, 1 - 3 hrs.
- Becoming a Winner, 75 minutes, 3 hours
- The Balancing Act (Work/home) 1 - 3 hours, 1 day
- Effective Letter Writing, 1 day
- Interpersonal Skills, 3 hours, 1 - 3 days
- Coping with Stress, 1 - 3 hours, 1 day *
- Dealing with Anger - Yours & Theirs, 3 hrs.
- Dynamic Goal Setting, 90 minutes or 1 day
- Time Management - For Supervisors or For Life,
    1 - 3 hours or 1 day
- Time & Stress Control, 3 hours, 1 day
- Managing Time, Stress & Difficult People, 1 ½ or 2 days
- Surviving Change (Receivers of) 3 - 6 hours

CAREER DEVELOPMENT

- Cracking the Glass Ceiling, 3 or 4 hours, 1 - 2 days
    (book available)
- Get That Job, 3 hours or 1 day
- Career Decisions - 1 & 2 days
- What Am I Going to Do With The Rest Of My Life? 1 day

HUMAN RESOURCES

- Managing the Human Resources Function, 2 days
- Employee Discipline, 3 hours or 1 day
- Hiring Know-How, 3 hours, 1 - 1 ½ days
- Easy Come - Hard to Go, 1 or 2 days
- Job Description & Performance Appraisals, 3 hrs. 1 day
- Train the Trainer, 1 day or 2 ½ days

SUPERVISORY/MANAGEMENT TRAINING

- Survival Skills for Supervisors/Managers,
  1, 2, 3, 5, and 13 day or 18 - 3 hour
- Team Building, 1 - 3 hours or 1 day
- Surviving Change, (Implementors) 3 - 6 hours
- Productive Meetings, 3 ½ hours or 1 day
- Creative Problem Solving, 3 & 4 hrs, 2 days

CLERICAL

- The Professional Secretary, 1 day
- Receptionist Training, 1 day
- Time Management for Support Staff, 1 day
- Critical skills for Executive Asstants 2 days
- Advanced Skills for Administrative Assistants 2 days
- Telephone communication skills
- Customer service

****

Presented by ROBERTA CAVA, president of Cava Management Consulting Services. She is the author of the best-selling books **DIFFICULT PEOPLE - How to Deal With Impossible Clients, Bosses and Co-workers** *(released in Canada, U.S.A. Great Britain, Europe, Asia, Middle East, Africa, Australia and New Zealand); and* **ESCAPING THE PINK-COLLAR GHETTO - How Women Can Advance in Business** *(released in Canada and France).*
       Soon to be released are:
DEALING WITH DIFFICULT RELATIVES & IN-LAWS;
DEALING WITH DIFFICULT FRIENDS AND NEIGHBOURS; AND
DEALING WITH DIFFICULT PROFESSIONAL AND TRADESPEOPLE